DECODING THE MATRIX: THE RESURRECTION OF OPHIUCHUS

EZEKIEL BRUMFIELD JR.

Copyright © 2017 EZEKIEL BRUMFIELD JR

All rights reserved.

ISBN: 978-0-692-08830-2

DEDICATION

This book is dedicated to my late grandfather Samuel Curtis (peace be with him). Weeks before his departure, he told me to "keep using your brain and pen." His words will stick with me for the rest of my life.

CONTENTS

Acknowledgments   i

Preface   ii

1	What is Astrology? Who Corrupted it?	Pg #1
2	Tropical vs. 13 Sign	Pg #6
3	Why is the 13th Sign Important?	Pg #12
4	Background of Ophiuchus	Pg #17
5	Elements, Qualities, and Genders	Pg #24
6	Sun Signs	Pg #29
7	Moon Signs	Pg #58
8	Ascendant	Pg #66
9	Mercury	Pg #73
10	Venus	Pg #81
11	Mars	Pg #89
12	Jupiter	Pg #97
13	Saturn	Pg #103
14	Uranus	Pg #109
15	Neptune	Pg #114
16	Pluto	Pg #119

17	Chiron	Pg #125
18	Midheaven	Pg #132
19	Using the Zodiac to Manifest	Pg #139
20	Compatibility	Pg #141
21	Business Astrology	Pg #145
22	Natal Charts	Pg #151
23	Houses	Pg #153
24	Astrological Transits	Pg #159
25	The True Astrological Age	Pg #161
	Bibliography	Pg #167
	About the Author	Pg #172

ACKNOWLEDGMENTS

First and foremost, I would like to thank God for guiding me, helping me use discernment, and sending real astronomical knowledge my way. Thank you mother and father, for raising me in a loving and mentally stimulating environment. I must also show gratitude to my grandmother and late grandfather (peace be with him) for sharing their wisdom and words of encouragement in times of need. I have to acknowledge my best friend Arnika as well. She was very supportive throughout the whole book writing process. I appreciate everyone who is reading this book and helping me spread astrological information that matches astronomy. This is a global effort.

Preface

One day I asked myself "Why doesn't tropical astrology match the sky?" I even asked others the same question. No one could give me an answer, so I denounced the tropical system and started my journey to higher knowledge. It wasn't until about 2013 when I purchased a telescope and started studying astronomy. I learned that astrology and astronomy were seen as one since the beginning of time. Eventually, I was led to the forgotten 13th sign named Ophiuchus. Ophiuchus is the hidden link between astrology and astronomy. A wise woman by the name of Femi gave me my first 13 sign astrological chart reading. She's an Ophiuchus sun herself. Her reading changed my life and inspired me to learn how to read natal charts, so that I could spread this knowledge to others. The Internet is flooded with information based on tropical astrology. On the other hand, astrological data including 13 signs is scarce, which is why I wrote this book. It will provide truth seekers with a solid foundation to start studying 13 sign astrology.

1. WHAT IS ASTROLOGY? WHO CORRUPTED IT?

"What's your sign?" is one of the most common ways to start a conversation. We hear of astrology from pop culture to magazines. A lot of people can't go a day without checking their horoscope. Many build their whole lives around it. The masses have watered down everything from science to spirituality. This includes astrology. Mainstream astrology is harmful because it isn't even astrology. It doesn't match the sky, so it's just another lie.

First, let's break down the meaning of astrology. Astro means "star" and ology means "the study of." That being said, astrology is the study of stars and its purest form is built on stargazing. Sidereal is another name for star based astrology. It simply means "star." 13 sign astrology is the purest form of sidereal. It's different from a lot of the sidereal systems that most people are used to. Astronomy and astrology were originally one. In the days of the ancient ones, the astronomer was also a mathematician and astrologer. Ancient astronomers used stars to plant crops, predict things, build structures, track time, identify seasons, measure distance, and navigate. The 3 wise men of the bible alluded to the 3 stars in Orion's belt, which point directly to Sirius. Alnitak, Alnilam, and Mintaka are the names of the 3 stars.

    Sirius is the brightest star in our night sky. Orion's belt is still used to pinpoint other stars today. Taurus and Gemini shine brightly as neighboring constellations. Observing cycles and patterns in nature is how ancient astronomers kept up with the natural order of things. Humans are not in tune with nature anymore. Most don't look up at the night sky and observe stars.

Forget about the system that majority deal with today. It is bad astronomy and deception. Modern astrology is based on false heavens and artificial time. This makes it devilish. We should be working with real planetary movements since we're microcosms of the universe experiencing itself. Everything is connected. If we sit and observe the heavens, we will learn a lot about life. The stars have their own language. Listen to them speak.

The atom that gave birth to stars and plants also gave birth to humans. We share similar energy and frequencies with all that exists. There are codes in the sky that one must study. Holy texts say, "The signs are in the sky." Constellations are hieroglyphs in the heavens. They tell stories about our origin. People believe the moon influences tides but don't acknowledge the influence heavenly bodies have on us. They seem to forget about the law "as above, so below."

Astrology can be traced back to ancient civilizations like Mesopotamia (Iraq) and Kemet (Egypt). The ancient Kemetics credited Djehuti aka Tehuti or Thoth for introducing astrology to the world as well as astronomy, medicine, magic, spirituality, religion, language, writing, math etc. He is known for building the ancient pyramids. They align with the stars and have existed on Earth for thousands of years. It took supreme mathematical and astronomical knowledge to build them.

Why do we separate astrology from astronomy? In about 100-150 AD, the Romans corrupted astrology and based it on seasons instead of stars. Ptolemy is the mathematician responsible for introducing tropical astrology. The Romans broke the zodiac wheel into 12 equal pieces. Sacred mathematics was too complex for them, so they had to simplify it. They also eliminated Ophiuchus because it is a woman. This helped them further their woman hating agendas. It adds up since 13 is the number of the goddess.

Ophiuchus represents the enlightened woman. Romans killed and enslaved women. They wanted to keep women as far away from their true power as possible. Removing Ophiuchus from the zodiac wheel helped them create a ton of confusion. They even changed the gender. The Romans fixed Aries to start spring since they were masculine lovers of war. Aries, the god of war, represents them perfectly.

Man corrupted astrology just like everything else. Corrupting astrology created fake time. Fake time creates fake frequencies. Fake frequencies keep people dumbed down and trapped in the matrix. They alter the mind of the masses, which makes society easier to control. Many question religion but don't question the tropical system. Question everything and you will find the answers.

2. TROPICAL VS. 13 SIGN

In the previous chapter, we learned that astrology is the study of stars. Mainstream astrology is called tropical because it is based on seasons rather than stars. The seasons are opposite in different hemispheres, which means the tropical system wouldn't have the same influence on the Northern Hemisphere as it has on the Southern Hemisphere. 13 sign astrology is based on real stars and constellations whether or not they can be seen from the Northern or Southern Hemisphere.

Pure astrology is metaphysical astronomy. It's beyond what limited human eyes see. We can go outside and actually observe current planetary movements with star based astrology. Nowadays, we don't even need telescopes because the stars are closer than ever. Anyone can download Google sky maps or other astronomical apps to track real planetary movements. The average person can easily debunk the tropical system by looking up at the night sky from rural areas. Stars are never where tropical fanatics believe them to be.

If you want to study the stars then the tropical system has no value to you. Everyone working with tropical natal charts is working with the wrong energy. That's why a lot of them are stagnant. They are missing out on potential opportunities and do not benefit from astrology in reality. The 13th sign is not new. We just were never claiming the right signs or working with real transits to begin with.

According to mainstream astrology, the spring equinox is fixed to Aries season. Astronomically speaking, Pisces starts spring. This is symbolic because Pisces and spring both deal with water. Another sign will eventually mark the spring equinox since everything is always shifting and evolving. Nothing is still.

Tropical astrologers believe the zodiac wheel is divided into 12 equal pieces. Astronomers know the sun enters 13 constellations on the ecliptic, which are all different shapes and sizes. The ecliptic is the path that the sun crosses. Different shapes and sizes create different degrees but tropical astrologers insist on believing that each sign is a simple 30 degrees. Astronomically speaking, Virgo is 45 degrees. It is also the biggest sign. Scorpio is 6.5 degrees, which makes it the smallest.

Tropical astrologers believe the sun enters each sign for a simple 30 days. The universe is more complex though. In reality, the sun is in Virgo for 45 days and Scorpio for only 6 days. This math goes against the 30 days rule of mainstream astrology. The sun doesn't have anything to do with months. It deals with years. Months actually come from the word moon and are based on measurements of moon cycles. The moon moves through each sign every 28 days to complete a cycle. This means that it spends a little over 2 days in each sign. The Romans removed the 13th sign and month.

Tropical astrology is 28 degrees (and counting) off from the real sky. That's equal to about one whole zodiac sign or moon cycle off. The tropical system will become more inaccurate over time. 13 sign astrology is built on real time and works with the 13-month lunar calendar. Mainstream astrology is based on flawed math while 13 sign astrology is mathematically and astronomically correct.

Ptolemy believed Earth was the center of the universe. Everyone knows this is incorrect. How can you still believe in the tropical system after finding out it's built on lies? Ophiuchus is the center of the universe in reality and has a supermassive dark hole within it. This makes the 13th sign significant. Tropical astrology is so ego based that most people only know about sun signs. The sun deals with the ego or personality. Many are obsessed with their false egos (false sun signs) and build their whole lives around them.

The position of the sun isn't the only thing that tropical astrology has incorrect. Tropical astrologers are wrong about the other planetary movements as well. They also ignore the changes and shifts Earth is going through. Even though tropical astrology was never right to begin with, astrology should evolve along with everything else. 13 sign astrology acknowledges the shifts and will continue to evolve with the rest of the cosmos.

If you have the choice to choose between right and wrong, why not make the right decision? One is factual and one is not. Our ancestors paid attention to the patterns and cycles in nature. Why don't we? They knew Ophiuchus would become a revelation in our sky thousands of years ago.

It's confusing seeing women work with mainstream astrology when men, who hate them, introduced it. Tropical astrology feeds into the patriarchal system that many women claim they want to destroy. This is extremely hypocritical. Women who are against patriarchy should be working with Ophiuchus to end deception.

3. WHY IS THE 13TH SIGN IMPORTANT?

It took us 2000 years to rediscover that astrology should be one with astronomy. Ophiuchus is the missing link that merges astrology (spirituality) with astronomy (science). It is also a portal bringing the world new information, frequencies, and codes. That's why it's hidden and won't resonate with most. The rulers of the world want to keep us tuned into low frequencies, so we can be easily controlled. The stars are alive and have messages for us to decode. Those using discernment will discover the secrets of the universe and tune in with the cosmic forces of Ophiuchus.

Ophiuchus (the 13th sign) is a symbol of rebirth. The shift in signs can be very beneficial since people like to cling to identities. We all must go through death and rebirth in order to reach our full potential. False identities hold us back. Ophiuchus couldn't have returned to the zodiac at a better time. Everyone needs this transformation. One must transcend from lower self to higher self. Ophiuchus is the true and evolving individual. This individual desires knowledge of higher planes and immortality. He or she wants to share truth with others and help them advance through the multidimensional shift of the ages. Ophiuchus is an eternal student of life.

It's vital for women to work with Ophiuchus, so that they can remember their true power. Ophiuchus represents the return of goddess energy and the matriarchal universe. Women play an important role in the great awakening. They are guardians of sacred knowledge, leaders of revolutions, lawmakers, mothers, teachers of humanity, healers etc. There is no evolution without evolving women. The rest of the world will follow their lead once they begin healing and raising their standards.

Ophiuchus sits in the center of the galaxy with a dark hole representing womb energy. The entire universe revolves around the womb. Women are healing their wombs and connecting with their bodies again. Womb energy will heal the world. Those in power know women will give birth to the saviors of humanity, so they are doing anything they can to prevent it, which is why the war on the womb exists.

Women are astronomical by nature. It's one reason a lot of them gravitate to modern astrology even though it's inaccurate. They were originally the keepers of calendric and astronomical knowledge. We can observe the menstrual cycle and see that it's linked to the moon. Women must work with Ophiuchus again. It connects humanity with the natural order of things.

Ophiuchus is the woman in tune with her full power.

She is not ashamed of being sensual, sexual, spiritual, intellectual, emotional etc. Ophiuchus is one with the water, animals, and forces of nature. This gives her the power to heal with herbs. She also has power over life and death. Women can't reach Ophiuchus level until they stop letting men demonize them for being their natural selves. That's where their true power lies. Ophiuchus is the fully empowered woman who intimidates man.

Ophiuchus will help humanity raise our consciousness levels and heal with the planet during this great alignment of worlds. Men can't connect with Ophiuchus until we start honoring women. We must learn to respect ourselves and heal how we view human sexuality. Animalistic views of sexuality hinder our progress. Sexuality is a powerful force when it's used properly instead of abused.

Sex can be used to raise consciousness levels, awaken

chakras, strengthen immune systems, decrease stress, increase intimacy, deepen our connection with the source etc. Ophiuchus symbolizes the power of harnessing sexual energy to manifest a greater life. We become Ophiuchus when we merge with the universe and master our lives on all levels. Most people only focus on the physical. Ophiuchus is multidimensional.

Ophiuchus is the alchemist and destroyer of false realities. Anyone breaking cycles in his or her family is working with Ophiuchus. They are the black sheep of their families. Ophiuchus energy will get rid of corruption, outdated paradigms, and old ways of living. It will help men and women heal the relationships we have with one another and harmonize the masculine and feminine energies within each of us. Ophiuchus is key to ascension. It's preparing us for the next evolutionary phase, which involves unlocking the divinity within.

4. BACKGROUND OF OPHIUCHUS

Ophiuchus is known as the Serpent Bearer. It's important to pronounce OF-EE-YOO-CUS correctly. The name itself is magic. Ophiuchus is a woman holding a snake. She symbolizes the one who has control over their kundalini or life force energy. Kundalini energy, like Ophiuchus is linked to immortality and serpents.

The Serpent Bearer has a connection with Imhotep, the father of medicine. Many know Hippocrates as the father of medicine but this is just another lie. Ophiuchus represents Asclepius. Chiron raised Asclepius and taught him the art of healing. This is why some people believe Chiron (the asteroid) rules Ophiuchus. Asclepius watched a serpent bring another serpent back to life with herbs, which led him to healing others with herbs and becoming immortal. Zues killed Asclepius because he learned the secrets of death. He didn't want Asclepius using his secrets to make humanity immortal.

The hospital traditionally uses the symbol of 2 snakes spiraling up a rod. It is called the "Caduceus." This symbol is often mistaken for the rod with 1 snake, which is called the "Rod of Asclepius." Doctors stole the medicine Rod of Asclepius from Ophiuchus. Physicians believe they have control over our life force. It is up to us to heal ourselves. We shouldn't have to depend on anyone to take care of our health. Each individual has the power to heal from within.

Ophiuchus holds the keys to immortality. In one myth, Set tore his brother Ausar's (Osiris) body into 14 pieces. Ausar's wife Auset (Isis) and sister Nebt-het (Nephthys) found 13 of the 14 pieces. This is alluding to Ophiuchus (the 13th sign) and Orion (the upcoming 14th sign). Orion is the opposite of Ophiuchus. Ophiuchus is known as "The Star Gate of God" and Orion is known as "The Star

Gate of Man " (Saulnier 30). Eventually, we will acknowledge Orion as a part of the zodiac. The sun rides its cusp between June 18th-20th. The stars only have to shift a little bit more for the sun to cross Orion on the ecliptic.

Another myth that alludes to Ophiuchus is when Auset tricked Ra into giving her his secret name. No one knew the secret name but Ra himself. The secret name was key to his power. Ra took the same path across the ecliptic everyday. Auset created a venomous serpent and placed it on his path.

Ra (the sun) was traveling on his path right before being bitten by the snake. He said the pain was unlike anything he had ever felt and knew he didn't create such a creature. His cry for help brought many healers around him. "Is it fire? Is it water? I burn. I shiver" (Murray 83). The fire represents Sagittarius and the water represents

Scorpio. Ophiuchus sits between these 2 signs. Some people think Ophiuchus is fire while others think it is water. Its element is ether, so it burns.

Ra said, "Call to me the children of the gods, they who have skill in healing, they who have knowledge of magic, they whose power reach to the heavens" (Murray 83). Ra (the sun) is talking about the constellation Ophiuchus, which deals with magic and healing. Auset is the only one who can heal him. She is a magician who uses herbs and words to heal.

Auset walked to where Ra was in pain. Before Auset removed the serpent, she asked Ra what was his true name. The secret name gave Auset power. This is alluding to the 13th sign because Ra is the sun traveling the ecliptic or path of the sun. Ophiuchus is the true name of the sun or missing sun sign and Auset is the Serpent Bearer.

Ophiuchus sits between the 8th and 9th house. They are the homes of Scorpio and Sagittarius. It merges Scorpio (sex) with Sagittarius (higher learning) to achieve enlightenment. Ophiuchus is the dark womb in the center of the galaxy. The 13th sign represents sexual healing. Sexual healing can change the world into a better place.

Ophiuchus represents Christ energy. It is Christ walking on water. I say this because Ophiuchus' foot is above Scorpio, which is a water sign. A lot of people miss the astrological knowledge in holy texts because they take things too literally. Ophiuchus (the healer) also stands on Scorpio (death) to symbolize conquering death and enemies.

Many believe the number 13 is unlucky. It is actually a divine and powerful number. 13 is the number of the goddess and moon cycle. There are 13 months in a lunar year and 13 weeks in each season. How many known chakras are there? 13. The human body has 13 major joints and the zodiac wheel has 13 constellations. 13 is the number of rebirth.

Add the 12 disciples plus Christ (Ophiuchus) and get 13. Christ was a healer like Ophiuchus. The Romans killed Christ and the 13th sign. The resurrection of Ophiuchus is the return of Christ. Medusa is the corrupted version of Ophiuchus. They are both women with serpents that men fear. Serpents shed their skin to represent wisdom, immortality, healing, and rebirth.

Dr. Sebi was born on November 26th, 1933. The sun is in healing Scorpio during that time. Scorpio season is right before Ophiuchus, so there is a high chance he had Ophiuchus in his chart. Dr. Sebi was a well-known healer, like Ophiuchus/Imhotep, who cured people of many diseases. He knew the secrets of immortality, so "The man" killed him before he could share them with the rest of the humanity. "The man" would lose a lot of power and money if everyone was immortal. History repeats itself all the time. It's time for new healers to step up and carry the torch.

Ophiuchus is bigger than a sign and constellation. It's a level of attainment. Even if we don't have planets in Ophiuchus, we should observe the house that it's in. Learn to work with Ophiuchus and the other 12 signs or energies. Work with Orion as well even though it is not officially a part of the zodiac yet. Ophiuchus is the monk and guardian of ancient secrets. She is the yogi and shaman of the zodiac. It should be everyone's goal to balance the feminine and masculine energies within, so we can become Ophiuchus. Anyone can achieve this through inner alchemy, meditation, yoga, holistic healing, overcoming obstacles, staying persistent, maintaining a high vibration, seeking truth etc.

5. ELEMENTS, QUALITIES, AND GENDERS

Most people are aware of 4 elements but there are actually 5. The 5 elements are earth, air, water, fire, and ether. Taurus, Virgo, and Capricorn are earth signs. They are practical, sensual, and materially driven. Earth symbolizes the senses. This gives earthy people super senses. They are the "grounded" people of the zodiac. Earth signs like to take their time. On the negative side, they can be materialistic and very surfaced level.

Gemini, Libra, and Aquarius are air signs. Air signs are the intellectuals and socializers of the zodiac. They have many ideas and crave mental stimulation. Air signs enjoy learning and communicating. Communication is how they share their ideas. On the negative side, they can be airheads and superficial. They need to work on being grounded.

Cancer, Scorpio, and Pisces are water signs. They are the ultra sensitive, spiritual, and emotional people of the zodiac. These people are feelers with a lot of depth and intensity to them. Some of them have psychic abilities. On the negative side, they can be easily manipulated emotionally. They have problems when it comes to creating boundaries. Water needs security or it will be all over the place.

Aries, Leo, and Sagittarius are fire signs. People with a lot of fire are fast moving, assertive, aggressive, impulsive, enthusiastic, energetic, and high-spirited. They tend to be passionate, fun, independent, self-motivated, bossy, and hot tempered as well. These people need a lot of freedom and space or the flame becomes destructive. Fire signs are the movers, doers, and natural leaders of the zodiac. They desire a lot of stimulation and adventure, so they are always on the search for something new.

13 sign astrology reintroduces Ophiuchus and the ether element. Ophiuchus is the ethereal sign of the zodiac. Ether is spirit, so that makes Ophiuchus natives free-spirited and mental. Ether is the subtle yet powerful energy that makes up all of creation. It's everywhere and unseen. People like to ignore ether since it's intangible. Ether is a part of the other 4 elements. It's where they come from. The 5th element creates balance between them. It makes up the empty space that the other elements fill. Ether is formless, mysterious, expansive, and limitless. Ethereal signs aren't the most mechanically inclined. The physical world bores them. They enjoy figuring out how things work beyond the physical.

The zodiac wheel is divided into 3 qualities: mutable, fixed, and cardinal. Mutable signs start each season. They are changeable, impressionable, and adaptable. Pisces starts spring. Gemini starts summer. Virgo starts fall and Sagittarius starts winter. This urges us to make changes when we bring in the seasons. It's interesting how Virgo (the sign of harvest) symbolizes harvest season and Pisces (the Fish) symbolizes spring. Ophiuchus is known by many to be mutable. One day, it will start the winter season. Mutable signs are the finishers of the zodiac.

Taurus, Leo, Scorpio, and Aquarius are fixed signs. These people are firm, decisive, stable, and dependable. They are steady and determined to finish. Fixed signs take their time with everything. They are the builders and maintainers of the zodiac. On the negative side, they can be stubborn and resistant to change.

Aries, Cancer, Libra, and Capricorn are cardinal signs. Cardinal signs are considered the initiators and leaders of the zodiac. These people are known for starting things but aren't really fond at finishing them. Cardinal signs don't usually plan before they take action. They are quick, active, ambitious, and restless.

Signs are divided into genders or sexes. I know a lot of people don't like the terms gender or sex, so call these energies whatever makes you comfortable. There are feminine and masculine energies. Taurus, Cancer, Virgo, Scorpio, Ophiuchus, Capricorn, and Pisces are feminine. They are earth, water, and ethereal signs. Feminine signs are subjective, introverted, passive, shy, and inward. They are usually emotional and sensual.

Aries, Gemini, Leo, Libra, Sagittarius, and Aquarius are masculine signs. These are fire and air signs. They are active by nature, which makes them extroverted and outward. Masculine signs are interested in the things happening around them. They take action instead of being passive.

6. SUN SIGNS

Do not limit yourself to one sign. All of the signs are within us. We can work with any sign (energy) that we choose. I will discuss this matter further in chapter 19. When people ask, "What's your sign?" they are talking about sun signs. Sun signs are the most basic signs. They deal with personality. I like to refer to sun signs as the ego. Some people refer to them as the soul. A theory of mines is that we may have been stars in specific constellations before this lifetime. The stars are alive in the heavens. We ascend to the heavens and become stars again after we die. I have personal experiences to back up my views.

My grandmother was born on December 21st. She is a Sagittarius sun. Before she ascended, we had one last conversation about astrology. She said something about Sagittarius letting me know she was returning to her place in the stars. My grandmother ascended December 29th, 2015 during Sagittarius season. Instead of being sad, I look up at Sagittarius and smile because I know she is in a better place.

The sun tells us about our different characteristics and skills. It is masculine and represents the conscious self. My sun is in Gemini. This makes me intellectual, curious, communicative, and great at multitasking. I enjoy buying the newest gadgets and surfing the Internet. Growing up, I was a tech lover and scholar. My life is about learning as much as I possibly can.

DATES CAN SHIFT

Aries

April 18th-May 13th

Do you know an active, authoritative, pioneering, masculine, daring, and aggressive "Taurus?" Is he or she quick to start on projects but not so quick to finish them? That person is actually a martial, impatient, passionate, idealistic, driven, youthful, spontaneous, and independent Aries sun. Aries suns have a reputation for being mean, tough, and stubborn since they are linked to the god of war. They are the warriors of the zodiac.

Taurus is resistant to change. Aries, on the other hand, thrives on change. Taurus is also the laziest sign while Aries is always looking for action and adventure. Aries is known as the Ram and rules the head. Aries suns can be forceful and hot headed. The Rams will charge anyone they feel the need to. They must learn to control their anger, think before they act, and finish what they start. Aries suns are courageous go-getters who like to show off their accomplishments with nice cars and other material things. They enjoy competing, taking on challenges, experiencing new things, exploring new ideas, setting trends, and initiating new projects.

Materialistic Mars is the ruler of Aries and pleasure-loving Venus is the ruler of Taurus. Aries and Taurus suns are both materialistic, which is why there is so much confusion. Aries natives move too fast to mistake for Taurus suns. Taurus is a slow-moving earth sign. Aries suns can be bossy, selfish, blunt, and impulsive. Their selfishness is a result of them being the 1st of the zodiac. They have a strong need for individuality and can make great leaders. Aries is the Ram sand Taurus is the Bull. Rams are similar to bulls. They are both stubborn animals with horns. We can see why Aries think they are Taurus suns.

Taurus

May 14th - June 20th

Do you know any cautious, practical, sensual, stuck in their ways, reliable, and materially driven "Geminis?" They are really slow-moving Taurus suns. Geminis are great at multitasking while Taurus natives are not. They are more grounded and artistic than Geminis. Taurus natives love routine. Geminis, on the other hand, are bored by routine.

Taurus rules the senses and throat, which is why many Taurus natives are singers. They have powerful voices. This is one reason Taurus suns think they are communicative Geminis. They enjoy good food, drinks, music, and beautiful surroundings since pleasure-loving Venus rules Taurus. The material plane is the Bull's strong point. Taurus suns aren't all that into the mental plane like true Geminis. With that said, they can fall victim to self-indulgence, greed, and materialism.

Taurus suns are persistent, patient, and determined to carry everything through. Taurus is the sign of values. They enjoy the luxuries of life and anything valuable. Being rewarded for their work is important. Taurus natives value security, structure, and stability more than Geminis. It's important for them to establish spiritual values or they will focus only on the material world. They must learn to live unattached to their possessions.

Taurus suns are too slow moving, single-minded, stubborn, and inflexible to confuse themselves with Geminis. They do not change easily. Repeating the same lessons over and over again is very common for the Bull. Imbalanced Taurus suns are known for lying since they are throat ruled. People mistakenly call them Geminis all the time, which is why Geminis have such a bad reputation.

Gemini

June 21st - July 19th

Do you know any logical, witty, flexible, detached, quick on their feet, and always on the go "Cancers?" They are definitely Geminis. Geminis are more intellectual, social, and communicative than Cancers. They are the Twins and social butterflies of the zodiac while Cancers are true homebodies. Geminis make great conversationalists. It's not the moon that makes them moody. The Twins deal with duality. One twin is social and the other is private. Geminis are always switching from feminine to masculine sides of the brain. This makes them lovers of variety. Routine bores them.

Mercury rules Gemini. It is known as the trickster and messenger. Both nicknames describe the Twins accurately. Geminis love the Internet, gadgets, trade, and media. They can make great mass communicators and internet entrepreneurs. Mercury is the planet of short travel. Geminis love to move around. Traveling is healing to them. Geminis are usually great at multitasking. They may end up being "jacks of all trades, masters of none" if they are not careful. Geminis are too detached and logical to be confused with moody Cancers. They must learn to control their mind.

Clever and curious Geminis are always on a journey to learn. They are the "brainiacs" of the zodiac. Gemini is linked to the hands, shoulders, and lungs. They can be very skilled with their hands, which makes them great writers and musicians. The Twins reflect changes in their surroundings and camouflage very well. Imitation is something they do effortlessly. On the negative side, they can be nosey, conniving, gossipy, mischievous, unreliable, superficial, scattered, changeable, impressionable, and indecisive.

Cancer

July 20th - August 9th

Do you know any emotional, maternal, unpredictable, sensitive, sentimental, and family-oriented "Leos?" They are actually homebody Cancers and not as fiery as they believe. A lot of Cancer males are gentlemen, which is why they mistake themselves for romantic Leos. Cancers are a little more caring and selfless than Leos. Leos can be very self-centered.

The watery moon rules Cancer instead of the blazing sun. Cancers are more empathetic and compassionate than Leos. On the negative side, they can be moody, crabby, possessive, clingy, and impressionable. These natives have the ability to channel their intense emotions into creativity. Cancers must learn to give their loved ones the freedom to be who they are, create boundaries, and stop clinging to the past. They tend to themselves in their shell a lot, which is why they are known as the Crabs of the zodiac. Self-preservation is important to them. They take on the energy of others easily.

Cancers are connected to the breast and likely to be into some type of caretaking work. They are more passive than aggressive and assertive Leos. Cancers are the mothers of the zodiac. They love to nurture their loved ones and build homes. Cancers may like to share their love life with their family and friends since they have close bonds with them. They can be dramatic when it comes to expressing emotions. This is probably why some see them as dramatic Leos.

The Crab is protective of its family like the Lion. Cancer is a cardinal sign, which makes the Crab a leader in its own way. This is another reason Cancers confuse themselves with action-oriented Leos. They may seem gentle and passive but they are getting things done.

Leo

August 10th - September 15th

Do you know any self-centered, assertive, energetic, bossy, and dramatic "Virgos?" These people are really fiery, independent, and risk-taking Leos. They rather boss people around than serve them. Leos are bossy while Virgos are more about service. They are the muscle. Leos can make great managers and businessmen or women because of their ambition. The Lion is the symbol for Leo. Leos are the drama queens and kings of the zodiac. They are creative, strong-willed, fun loving, charismatic, and entertaining individuals.

Leos are aggressive, blunt, and direct like the other fire signs. They are fierce when it comes to speaking their mind. Leo is connected to the heart, which makes balanced Leos some of the most romantic and loving people on the planet. Like a lion, Leos are courageous, proud, and protective over their loved ones. On the negative side, they can be prideful, attention seeking, hot headed, and arrogant.

The sun rules Leo, so they feel like the world revolves around them. Leos are the celebrities of the zodiac. They stand out from the crowd. Leos like to make good first impressions and receive admiration from others. Their personality is strong, warm, sunny, huge, and expressive. They must learn to control their ego and express themselves from the heart in order to develop a healthy identity. Creative self-expression is their gift. They must learn to stop trying to control others. Self-mastery will bring them fulfillment. Leos have a special connection with children. They can make great leaders, bosses, actors, entertainers, artists, and sports players.

Virgo

September 16th - October 30th

Do you know any detailed-oriented, organized, and practical "Libras?" They are in fact earthy Virgos. Virgos are the workaholics of the zodiac. They love to serve and feel productive. The sun is in Virgo the longest, which makes most of the world's population Virgos. Virgo is known as the goddess of justice and the Scales also deal with justice. We can see why most Virgos feel like peace-loving Libras.

Virgos are the perfectionists of the zodiac. They need to learn that nothing is perfect. One of their lessons is to stop trying to perfect people. Virgos are the biggest critics. They can be highly critical of others and themselves. Self-improvement is important to them. Virgo is linked to health and the digestive system, so Virgos must make sure that they take care of their health.

They feel like Libras because they are analytical and intellectual. This comes from their connection to Mercury.

Virgos are very visual natives. They love order, cleanliness, and routine. Virgos are some of the freshest when it comes to fashion sense and style since they pay attention to detail very well. They can easily be stylists or photographers. Virgos love nature. A lot of them work with animals.

Virgo and Scorpio are sister signs, which is why a few Virgos believe they are Scorpios. It makes sense why the symbols of Virgo and Scorpio both look like the letter "M." Virgo's symbol has a tail that goes inward. This describes how Virgos radiate sexual energy. The Virgins radiate their sexual energy inwards. Scorpio's symbol has a tail that goes outward to represent sexual organs. Scorpions radiate their sexual energy outwards. This is why Scorpios are known for being sexual while Virgos are known for being conservative. Virgo, Libra, and Scorpio constellations were once connected. It makes sense why Virgos think they are Libras and Scorpios.

Libra

October 31st - November 22nd

Do you know any social, artistic, charming, flirty, and beauty-loving "Scorpios?" They are definitely Libras. Libras are air signs, which makes them intellectual and not as emotional as watery Scorpios. Scorpios are private and aren't very social. Libras, on the other hand, like to socialize a lot. It's rare to find them alone. They are always on the scene and make great party hosts.

Libra and librarian aren't similar words for no reason. Libras are the storytellers of the zodiac. These natives are communicative like the other air signs. They make great writers. Scorpios are low key and inward while Libras are extroverted and outward by nature. Beauty-loving Venus rules Libra instead of dark and mysterious Pluto. Their love for pleasure can lead to self-indulgence.

Libra deals with 7th house things like marriage, romance, and relationships. It's known as the sign of relationships and the Scales. Libras try their hardest to balance all of their relationships. On the negative side, they may feel like they need a relationship or need to be around people. The Scales deal with fairness, peace, harmony, balance, and weighed options. Libras can be people pleasers and indecisive at times. They see both sides of every situation, which makes them great at compromising.

Libra was once considered the Claws of Scorpio, so we can see why Libras confuse themselves with Scorpios. Libra was also known as the Scales of Virgo. The Scales are always trying to find balance between their Virgin and Scorpion energies. An overly emotional and secretive Libra is more on the Scorpion side while a conservative and earthy Libra is more on the Virgin side.

Scorpio

November 23rd - November 28th

Do you know a mysterious, passionate, low-key dominant, and unaffected "Sagittarius?" That person is a true Scorpio. Scorpios value privacy. They are quiet and reflective in crowds while Sagittarius suns are loudmouths. Scorpios are introverted by nature. The genitals rule them, so they are highly sexual beings. This is one reason Scorpios are known for becoming sex addicts. Immature Scorpios misuse their sexual energy. Scorpios become intensely involved with the people they bond with, which can lead to emotional attachments.

Mysteries, sex, death, psychology, rebirth, and the secrets of nature intrigue Scorpios. They are the secretive and emotional investigators of the zodiac. People like to limit Scorpio energy to sexual energy but it is also healing, creative, and transformative. Scorpios go through a lot of transformations throughout life. Scorpio is linked to the Scorpion and Pluto. This is why Scorpio seems so far out. The farthest known planet in our solar system rules it. Trauma seems to follow Scorpios wherever they go. Since the sun is only in Scorpio for 6 days, Scorpios embody the rarest energy in the world.

Scorpio is known to have several symbols. I will briefly discuss the most popular ones. The first symbol is the Scorpion. It is the least evolved version and experiences the darkest emotions. The Scorpion is power hungry, jealous, manipulative, judgmental, and possessive. The Eagle is the more evolved and spiritual version. It is less power hungry with a higher perspective. The Phoenix is the most developed version of Scorpio. It observes more and judges less. The Phoenix burns the old self to ashes to create a more purified version. This is where Scorpio finds peace.

Ophiuchus a.k.a. Serpentarius

November 29th - December 18th

Do you know a taboo loving, system destroying, curious, unconventional, mysterious, and hungry for truth "Sagittarius?" That person is certainly an Ophiuchus sun. Ophiuchus natives feel beyond social norms and hate rules. They love going against the grain and learning about secrets, conspiracies, astrology, psychology, magic, herbs etc. Ophiuchus suns love power and have the ability to speak anything into existence. They are rebellious and intense. Only a few can deal with organized religion. Some of them like to dress extravagantly in vibrant colors.

Ophiuchus is a woman holding a serpent. Some Ophiuchus natives like snakes. Men fear Ophiuchus. Ophiuchus suns are mistreated for no reason like Christ. Authorities usually respect Ophiuchus, which is why they level up quickly in their work fields. The element of Ophiuchus is ether, the 5th element. Ophiuchus is a mental sign, meaning these natives like to see things from beyond the veil. The Serpent Bearer is a mixture of transformative Scorpio and freedom-loving Sagittarius. Ophiuchus suns are fiery, passionate, changeable, and emotional. They may be interested in polygamy and sacred sexuality. On the negative side, they can be possessive and jealous.

Ophiuchus is the healer. Natives with this sun are usually interested in holistic health and herbal medicine. They may also be drawn to astrology and dream interpretation. Ophiuchus and Sagittarius are both linked to medicine but Ophiuchus natives are more likely to study natural medicine instead of going the traditional route. Some Ophiuchus suns, like Christ, leave their families at an early age.

Sagittarius

December 19th - January 18th

Do you know any philosophical, blunt, wild, energetic, athletic, spontaneous, passionate, social, and fast-moving "Capricorns?" They are really free-spirited Sagittarius suns. Sagittarius is known as the Archer. It's represented by a bow and arrow aimed upwards. Sagittarius natives are always aiming high, seeking a higher purpose, and being optimistic. Their enthusiasm and optimism is contagious. Sagittarius suns are more focused on freedom and possibilities than structure loving Capricorns. They move too much to be mistaken for slow and steady earth signs. Sagittarius suns are the wanderers and nomads of the zodiac.

Capricorns want to control their lives while Sagittarius suns rather go with the flow. Sagittarius rules the 9th house. This is the house of higher learning.

Everyday is a journey filled with learning and broadening horizons for them. They are students of life and philosophers. Sagittarius natives see the bigger picture. They love exploring other cultures, philosophy, challenges, fun, and traveling. The Archers make great teachers and channels of wisdom.

Sagittarius suns are fiery, so they like to move around a lot. They are the truth tellers of the zodiac and come across as blunt to everyone. Many are known for having loud mouths. On the negative side, they can be honest to a fault, argumentative, and arrogant. Sagittarius is depicted as half human and half horse (Centaur) and Capricorn is depicted as half goat and half fish. They are both 2 different species in one. This is one reason the Archer may feel like the Sea Goat. The Archers tend to juggle many projects and interests at once, which make them good at multitasking.

Capricorn

January 19th - February 15th

Do you know a slow and steady "Aquarius" who isn't too fond of science and technology? That person is without doubt a slow-moving Capricorn. Capricorns are more traditional and stable than Aquarius suns. They are focused and hardworking with good levels of concentration. Success, power, and status are most likely important to them.

The Sea Goat symbolizes Capricorn. It's a goat with a fish tail. This represents the dual nature of Capricorn. The mountain goat symbolizes the material and ambitious side. It climbs carefully and cautiously. The fish tail represents intuition, passion, imagination, spirituality etc. Capricorns achieve their desires by expressing who they are as souls. We can see why Capricorns confuse themselves with the Water Bearers.

They both deal with water but are not water signs.

Capricorns are connected to Saturn, so they tend to be organized, conservative, serious, disciplined, and time oriented. Sometimes, they can isolate themselves. Their patience, ambitious, and good planning skills will take them far. They aren't into taking shortcuts. Capricorn is the father and disciplinarian of the zodiac. The Sea Goats are more sensual, cautious, and structured than rebellious Aquarius suns. Capricorns like to enforce rules and Aquarius suns like to break them.

Aquarius natives embrace change while Capricorns do not. Many perceive Capricorns as cold and detached. They believe in keeping their emotions separate from work and relationships. This is another reason they are mistaken for Aquarius suns. Capricorn is the most detached earth sign. On the negative side, they can be stubborn, pessimistic, arrogant, materialistic, and lazy.

Aquarius

February 16th - March 11th

Do you know a detached, progressive, blunt, and unemotional "Pisces?" He or she is actually an observant, experimental, original, inventive, eccentric, curious, independent, creative, mysterious, and intellectual Aquarius sun. Aquarius lacks the sensitivity of Pisces. Aquarius is unconventional since it is connected to Uranus. Aquarius suns are often seen as rebellious because they like to make their own rules. They may be interested in science, research, technology, and the Internet. The Internet is Aquarius ruled. Aquarius natives are futuristic thinkers who enjoy contributing changes to humanity and observing human interactions. They desire new systems.

Aquarius is too logical and scientific to be confused with Pisces. It's known as the Water Bearer. The Water

Bearer is symbolically pouring water of life and spiritual nourishment into the world. This is one reason Aquarius natives are drawn towards different groups of people. Group relationships are important to them. They are here to baptize others with their truth. Aquarius natives may have different groups of friends for their wide range of interests.

Aquarius is also known as the god of storms, so it makes sense why it is mistaken for a water sign. Aquarius natives' lives are usually filled with unexpected changes, which is another reason they may believe they are mutable Pisces suns. The Water Bearer and the Fish both have huge imaginations combined with strong intuition. Aquarius natives gravitate to unorthodox religious and spiritual views while Pisces tend to be traditional. On the negative side, they can lack groundedness, practicality and empathy.

Pisces

March 12th - April 17th

Do you know an artistic, romantic, affectionate, selfless, and sensitive "Aries?" That person is definitely a dreamy, imaginative, inspiring, mystical, and intuitive Pisces sun. Pisces suns are more focused on inward than outward. Pisces is associated with dreams, which is why Pisces natives may have prophetic and vivid dreams. On the negative side, they can spend too much time daydreaming and procrastinating. Many of them suffer from a victim mentality or the lack of confidence, which leads to escapism and drug abuse. Pisces suns are too moody, compassionate, empathetic, selfless, gentle, and passive to be selfish fire signs.

Pisces likes to go with the flow of things and Aries likes to take control. Two fish symbolize Pisces because it deals with duality. One fish is going upstream and the other is going downstream. It's like two opposite personalities in one body. Pisces switches from being social and assertive to being introspective and passive easily. This makes Pisces suns very versatile.

Pisces natives may have grown up in religious households since Pisces rules the 12th house. The 12th house deals with spirituality, the subconscious, and religion. They can be too dreamy and idealistic when it comes to others. This causes them to be preyed on. They must learn how to create boundaries, see the divinity in all, and balance the spiritual with the physical. The Fish can take on the energy of others around them easily, so it's important for them to make time for solitude and meditation. It helps recharge their energy. They tend to lose themselves in the world. Pisces natives have the ability to tap into unseen forces. Some of them even have psychic abilities.

7. MOON SIGNS

Moon signs deal with the instinctual mind and emotions. The moon is feminine and associated with Cancer. Some people believe the moon is more important than the sun. It deals with the needs of a person. What comforts them? Moon signs help people understand how they express themselves, what makes them angry, and what makes them feel fulfilled. The moon is the most inner self. What does a person fear? How do they handle their emotions and react to things?

The moon itself influences a person's mood. Women even have cycles based on moon cycles. Unfortunately, many want to control their cycles or get rid of them. They are unaware of their sacred connection with nature. Moon signs play out in intimate relationships. They tell a person what they need from relationships and how they like to be nurtured. Moon signs are determined by the location of the moon at the time of one's birth.

Moon in Aries

Moon in Aries natives are the independent type. These people feel happiest when they are left to do their own thing. They express their emotions quickly. That makes them quick tempered, impatient, and impulsive. Independent and exciting people attract them.

Moon in Taurus

Moon in Taurus natives are sensual, reliable, romantic, and stable. They find comfort and security in the material plane. Taurus moons enjoy good food, music, drinks, and other worldly pleasures. On the negative side, they can be materialistic, self-indulgent, and inflexible. These natives are attracted to solid and reliable individuals.

Moon in Gemini

Gemini moons love mental stimulation. Communication is important to them. They like to converse about a variety of topics. Their lovers must keep their minds stimulated to keep them interested. Gemini moons are emotionally detached and like to intellectualize their emotions. On the negative side, they can be indecisive since they are always switching from one twin to another. This causes them to constantly deal with changing emotions. They have a very active mind, which can cause overloads sometimes.

Moon in Cancer

The moon is at home in Cancer. Cancer moons are ultra sensitive, moody, emotional, empathetic, clingy, family oriented, and intuitive. They find comfort through nurturing others and being nurtured. Cancers dislike confrontation and enjoy creating safe homes. They find it difficult to let go of people and things from their past.

Moon in Leo

Moon in Leo natives are dramatic, romantic, warm, and self-centered. Being acknowledged for their deeds is how they find comfort. They seek emotional validation from others because they feel like the world revolves around them. Leo moons can be arrogant and prideful.

Moon in Virgo

Moon in Virgo natives are analytical with their emotions. They tend to overthink. These people can be critical of themselves and others. This leads to perfectionism and nagging. Comfort is found through routine and work. Virgo moons can turn into workaholics. They are attracted to hardworking, attentive, and somewhat health-conscious individuals.

Moon in Libra

Libra moons are big on equality and justice. They are comfortable when their life is beautiful and balanced. Partnership makes them feel secured. On the negative side, they can feel like they need to be in a relationship. Moon in Libra natives are usually diplomatic, artistic, peacemaking, and social. Artistic people attract them.

Moon in Scorpio

Moon in Scorpio natives are intense, sexual, moody, intuitive, and emotional. Mysterious people attract them. They like to find emotional fulfillment through others. On the negative side, they can be obsessive, controlling, and secretive. Scorpio moons are more comfortable with death and taboos than others.

Moon in Ophiuchus a.k.a. Serpentarius

Moon in Ophiuchus natives have intense and changeable emotions. Some of them are androgynous and secretive of their sexuality. They may seek emotional nourishment and inspiration from women. Ophiuchus moons are geniuses. They can be master manipulators. Unconventional people attract them. They find comfort in going against the grain, figuring things out, shunning reality, and studying the unknown.

Ophiuchus moons are usually in touch with their inner goddess. They can cast spells and heal with herbs. This is witch doctor energy. Ophiuchus is the goddess who knows the secrets of life and death. Auset and Nebt-het are 2 sides of the moon. Auset is life and Nebt-het is death. The sisters saved Ausar when he was cut into pieces. Ophiuchus moons can be called on during a crisis.

Moon in Sagittarius

Sagittarius moons love freedom, adventure, and learning. They want to explore. Their optimistic and enthusiastic nature is contagious. They are on a quest of higher truth and understanding. Moon in Sagittarius natives find comfort through gaining higher knowledge and learning their place in the universe. Philosophy and foreign cultures interest them.

Moon in Capricorn

Moon in Capricorn natives are slow, grounded, responsible, calm, and collective. They come across as serious a lot of the time. Many view them as cold and detached but they are really just cautious with their feelings. Moon in Capricorn natives express their feelings with discipline. Mature and materially driven people attract them.

Moon in Aquarius

Moon in Aquarius natives are cold and detached when it comes to emotions. They feel too cool for lower emotions. These natives enjoy observing and studying human nature. Aquarius moons are social but rather be alone. They are unpredictable and unconventional. Independence and freedom make them comfortable. Mentally stimulating and unique people attract them.

Moon in Pisces

Moon in Pisces natives are sensitive, intuitive, emotional, compassionate, and artistic dreamers by nature. Since Pisces deals with duality, it's important for them to learn about boundaries. Pisces moons are considered old souls. Their dreams can be prophetic and vivid. They should avoid escapism. Spiritual and compassionate individuals attract them.

8. ASCENDANTS

Ascendant signs, according to mainstream astrology, are incorrect like the other star signs. The ascendant is the zodiac sign ascending above the eastern horizon during a native's birth. It's linked to the 1st house, which is the house of self. The ascendant is the first thing that people see when they meet someone. It is the side that people willingly show to the public and deals with everything from appearance to attitude. Some call it a mask but that would make it fake. The ascendant is what the family and environment conditions a person to behave like. It's best to look at it as a protective shell or external self. Ascendants are also known as rising signs. They can have more influence in a native's chart than sun signs.

Aries Ascendant

Aries ascendants view life as a challenge. They express themselves as active, innovative, independent, spontaneous, and assertive individuals. Many may perceive them as aggressive or bossy. They were probably labeled "independent" kids growing up.

Taurus Ascendant

Taurus ascendants approach life in a slow, steady, grounded, and patient manner. People see them as beauty loving, sensual, and charming. They like to wear the finest clothing and jewelry since they place a lot of value on material items. Self-indulgence can be a weakness.

Gemini Ascendant

Gemini ascendants express themselves in a witty and intellectual way. They can be too talkative. Geminis need many projects going on at once or they feel bored. This makes them great at multitasking. They are always looking for new opportunities to learn.

Cancer Ascendant

Cancers like to express themselves as nurturing, gentle, emotional, and family-oriented people. They enjoy taking care of others and being taking care of. Cancers feel safe at home since they are homebodies. They are sensitive to their environment.

Leo Ascendant

Leo ascendants view life as a huge creative project. They are dramatic, sunny, enthusiastic, warm, confident, generous, courageous, fun-loving, protective, proud, and powerful individuals. Leos like to be the center of attention. On the negative side, they can be prideful, attention seeking, and egotistical. They make great leaders and bosses.

Virgo Ascendant

Virgos come across as earthy, practical, and responsible. These ascendants are organized, detailed oriented, and probably somewhat health conscious. They can be workaholics. Being of service to others helps them feel fulfilled. Virgos may have been conditioned to be neat freaks or hypercritical.

Libra Ascendant

Libras are diplomatic, charming, intellectual, and social lovers of justice. Balance, harmony, beauty, and peace are important to them. On the negative side, Libras feel like they need to be around people. They find fulfillment through connecting with others.

Scorpio Ascendant

Scorpio ascendants are emotional, intense, investigative, and secretive with a strong presence. They have a lot sexual energy that must be released constructively. Scorpios grow emotional attachments to others and have a strong need to control their environment. This can cause possessiveness. They value privacy and like to seem unaffected by emotion.

Ophiuchus a.k.a. Serpentarius Ascendant

Ophiuchus ascendants are unpredictable, sexually magnetic, intense, and changeable. They may feel mistreated because they radiate feminine and powerful Medusa/Ophiuchus vibrations that men fear. Ophiuchus risings like to understand how the world works. They may dress flamboyantly. Some come across as androgynous. Herbs and magic may interest them.

Sagittarius Ascendant

Sagittarius ascendants are philosophical, freedom loving, and active. It's hard for them to keep still. They take an optimistic and enthusiastic approach to life. Sagittarius ascendants are always looking for an adventure. They may want to spend their lives traveling and learning from different cultures.

Capricorn Ascendant

Capricorn ascendants approach life in a slow, calm, and steady manner. Such people come across as patient, serious, ambitious, conservative, determined, mature, solid, earthy, reliable, practical, responsible, disciplined, and organized. They may have adopted a strong sense of tradition and responsibility at an early age. Success and public image are important to them. They are not afraid of working hard to achieve.

Aquarius Ascendant

Aquarius ascendants are intellectual, detached, rebellious, and unconventional in their approach to life. They love gadgets and face many unexpected changes throughout life. These people have always felt different growing up. Aquarius natives are great at observing and may be drawn to large groups of people. They are humanitarian with futuristic visions for humanity.

Pisces Ascendant

Pisces ascendants approach life in a passive and compassionate way. They come across as artistic, dreamy, imaginative, and peace-loving individuals. These natives like to go with the flow and aren't too big on detail. The Fish must learn to be more direct and objective or they will be taken advantage of. Art, religion, and spirituality may interest them.

9. MERCURY

Mercury is another celestial object mainstream astrology is lying about. It is the planet of logic and communication. Mercury also deals with trade and commerce. It helps people understand how they learn. Mercury is the messenger of the gods, so it explains how people express themselves and communicate as well. It rules earthy Virgo and airy Gemini.

Mercury in Aries

Mercury in Aries natives think and communicate in an impulsive, blunt, passionate, and direct manner. They can be bossy and forceful. These natives learn quickly through experience and like to be intellectually challenged. They are quick and impatient decision makers with minds full of ideas. People with Mercury in Aries are intellectually competitive and aggressive.

Mercury in Taurus

Mercury in Taurus natives may speak and write in a slow manner. They take their time with decision-making. Traditional knowledge is important to them. They are patient, hands on learners with good powers of concentration and plenty of common sense. Mercury in Taurus natives learn best through the senses in secured environments. They can be stubborn when others do not agree with their opinions and point of views. These people may fear learning new things.

Mercury in Gemini

Mercury is at home in Gemini. These natives are fast learners, great communicators, and witty with their words. They love to express themselves verbally and through writing. Mercury in Gemini natives are auditory learners, meaning they learn well through reading, lectures, and audio. They can make great writers or work in the media. Geminis enjoy the Internet and technology in general. On the negative side, they can be too talkative and easily bored. They are happiest in mentally stimulating environments.

Mercury in Cancer

Mercury in Cancer natives rely more on emotions than logic. They communicate in an empathetic, gentle, and sensitive way. Cancers learn best when they are emotionally balanced. They like feeling things out which makes them great listeners. Mercury in Cancer natives can easily read the emotions of others during conversations. They need nurturing, safe, and comfortable environments to learn and study in. These natives tend to have incredible memories.

Mercury in Leo

Mercury in Leo natives speak with authority. Some may come across as opinionated know-it-alls. They are excellent in getting their message across and can be very blunt. Leos take pride in their beliefs and will defend them. Creativity is important to them. Leos speak and write from the heart. They can be magnificent storytellers since they are dramatic. Mercury in Leo natives learn best through experience and adventure.

Mercury in Virgo

Mercury is at home in Virgo. Mercury in Virgo natives tend to be critical thinkers and hands on learners like the other earth signs. They are focused on the practical things in life and pay attention to detail very well. Time is important to them. Mercury in Virgo natives need orderly environments to learn and study in.

Mercury in Libra

Mercury in Libra natives are natural diplomats and great debaters. They are good at ceasing conflict and learn best through making connections. These people can be indecisive since they are always weighing their options. Mercury in Libra natives need balanced, stimulating, peaceful, and harmonious environments to learn and study in.

Mercury in Scorpio

Mercury in Scorpio natives use their curious minds to get to the bottom of things. They can pick up on the moods and vibes of others with ease. These people are investigators and problem solvers. They communicate in a passionate way. Mercury in Scorpio natives are fearless when it comes to exploring what no one else wants to explore or even think. They prefer to learn alone.

Mercury in Ophiuchus a.k.a. Serpentarius

Mercury in Ophiuchus natives are original and unpredictable spellbinders. They have the power to speak anything into existence. Their words can cause society to crumble. These natives are geniuses and potential tricksters. They love to research, mock authority, and go against conventional wisdom. Conventionality bores them. Rules aren't their thing. They rather create their own. Sciences like astronomy attract them. There is a tendency to intellectually dominate others.

Mercury in Sagittarius

Mercury in Sagittarius natives are natural salesmen. They communicate in an optimistic manner and don't hesitate to tell the truth. Their ideas are big. They enjoy expanding their horizons through traveling and studying subjects like philosophy. Their thirst for knowledge is undeniable even if they don't care for academics. These people learn best when they are given the freedom to think for themselves and experience life.

Mercury in Capricorn

Mercury in Capricorn natives communicate in a practical and authoritative way. They are conventional thinkers. These natives can't handle too much information coming at them all at once, so they break down information into pieces or blocks. They may write and speak in a slow and traditional manner. Mercury in Capricorn natives have good mental discipline. They love to learn alone in an orderly and traditional fashion.

Mercury in Aquarius

Mercury in Aquarius natives express themselves in an intellectual and unconventional manner. They love breaking the rules and being free thinkers. Mercury in Aquarius natives are detached individuals with minds full of innovative ideas. They learn best when they don't have to follow schedules because of their unusual study habits. People with this placement are auditory learners like the other air signs.

Mercury in Pisces

Mercury in Pisces natives have intuitive and imaginative minds. These people aren't too big on detail but make good listeners. They are driven more by intuition than facts. The Fish feel what others think. They learn best by absorbing information and observing the world around them. Mercury in Pisces natives communicate in a gentle, poetic, vague, and indirect way. This often leads to miscommunication. Music and art attracts them.

10. VENUS

Venus is the Roman goddess and planet of love. It tells one what they love, who they love, and how they like to be loved. Venus is also materialistic and feminine, so it deals with money as well. The planet of love tells people how they approach relationships and what they value. It is associated with Taurus and Libra.

Venus in Aries

Venus in Aries natives like to be in charge and hate to be bored. They don't really care for taking orders from others. People with this placement seem to enjoy a challenge and good chase. This can cause problems. They need plenty of adventure and stimulation or they will get bored. Fresh starts and new scenes are important to them. Aries aren't afraid to make the 1st move and go after who or what they want. They like to lead in love.

These people probably enjoy playing sports and exercising with their partners.

Venus in Taurus

Venus is at home in Taurus. Venus in Taurus natives enjoy the luxuries that life has to offer. They love to seek pleasure through good food, music, and drinks. This makes them sensual lovers. Taurus natives don't like to be rushed, so they take their time with love. They look for security, comfort, and stability in relationships.

Venus in Gemini

Venus in Gemini natives love to talk. Communication and learning are important to them. They need mental stimulation in relationships or they will get bored. These people crave variety, social lives, and constant change. This can cause commitment issues.

Venus in Cancer

Venus in Cancer natives like to nurture and feel nurtured. They are sensitive in love. Security, comfort, care, and emotional connections are important to them. In relationships, they like to feel safe. They are empathetic, nurturing, protective, and cautious. These individuals enjoy cuddling and affection. On the negative side, they can be clingy, possessive, and attached.

Venus in Leo

Venus in Leo natives are romantic, warm, and creative. They like for their significant others to boost their ego with compliments and gifts. Leos like to brag on their loved ones and expect them to do the same. They are dramatic and extravagant lovers who crave admiration from their partners. Venus in Leo natives love to keep the spark alive in relationships.

Venus in Virgo

Venus in Virgo natives are cautious, practical, and analytical when it comes to love. They don't rush into relationships. Venus in Virgo natives can be very critical and picky in relationships since Virgo is the perfectionist of the zodiac. They are always finding fault in others. Virgos like to serve their loved ones and express their love through practical means.

Venus in Libra

Venus is at home in Libra. Venus in Libra natives love beauty and art. Relationships are important to them. They are gentle lovers who enjoy connecting with others. On the negative side, they dislike being alone. This can cause them to be people pleasers. They like to be treated fairly since they believe in justice and balance. Libras enjoy sharing and communicating with their lovers.

Indecisiveness is a weakness. Therefore, they may have a hard time choosing a lover.

Venus in Scorpio

Venus in Scorpio natives are intense, emotional, fearless, sensitive, and passionate when it comes to love. On the negative side, they can be secretive, jealous, possessive, attached, and controlling. Commitment, depth, sexual pleasure, and emotional bonding please them in relationships. They give their partners their complete attention and even take things to extremes. Many of them are attracted to the darker side of reality.

Venus in Ophiuchus a.k.a. Serpentarius

Venus in Ophiuchus natives are intense and protective lovers. They can be power hungry, manipulative, possessive, secretive, and controlling in relationships. These natives like to dominate their lovers. People with Venus in Ophiuchus are probably into polygamy but can still be jealous in relationships. They seem cold but are the life of the party when they are around people they love and trust.

Venus in Sagittarius

Venus in Sagittarius natives are adventurous, optimistic, and freedom loving. They love fun. In love, they need to feel like they can broaden their horizons with their partners. Such people need a lot of freedom to grow or they will feel suffocated. They don't commit as easily as others. Venus in Sagittarius natives like exchanging philosophies, sharing ideas, and experiencing new things with their partners. They may enjoy traveling, exploring spirituality, looking into different cultures, and eating at foreign restaurants with their lovers.

Venus in Capricorn

Venus in Capricorn natives are slow, practical, cautious, and realistic when it comes to love. They like to take their time in relationships. These natives may even wait until they are successful to get in relationships. Venus in Capricorn natives are patient, reliable, and sensual. They are attracted to disciplined, serious, and goal oriented individuals. These people are conservative, committed, and consistent in relationships.

Venus in Aquarius

Venus in Aquarius natives take an unusual approach to love. They like to impress their lovers with their intellect and individuality. Mental stimulation and freedom are important to them. Their lovers have to be unusual, original, and progressive thinkers. Venus in Aquarius natives love to see others be their unique selves. They appreciate the Internet, unconventionality, science, and gadgets.

Venus in Pisces

Venus in Pisces natives are emotional, imaginative, peaceful, dreamy, romantic, passive, and empathetic partners. These people love deeply and enjoy feeling their love reciprocated. They are self-sacrificing in relationships, which can lead to being preyed on. Venus in Pisces natives are usually art lovers.

11. MARS

Mars is the material planet of action and Roman god of war. It is a masculine planet ruled by Aries. Mars deals with sex, desires, survival instincts, and drive. It shows how a person pursues their goals and passions. Are they aggressive? Do they have a high sex drive? What motivates them?

Mars in Aries

Mars in its home Aries is fiery, impatient, and aggressive with a hot temper. Aries natives are martial by nature. Being a winner motivates them. They enjoy initiating hot and passionate sex but don't usually last long. Sex is best when spontaneous and limitless. Mars in Aries natives should play sports and exercise to release this energy in a healthy way or it will burn them out. They might not finish what they start a lot of the time.

Mars in Taurus

Mars in Taurus natives are sensual and practical with a strong sexuality. Such people usually have a lot of stamina with high sex drives. They are slow and steady with good concentration. Mars in Taurus natives may not rush but they finish what they start. It takes them a while to become angry but once they reach that point, they become unexpectedly violent. They like to set the mood with food, drinks, and good music. Stability and security motivate them. This is a great placement for practicing sacred sexuality.

Mars in Gemini

Mars in Gemini natives like communication. Talking dirty gets them in the mood. They need mental connections with their sex partners. Geminis must have two or more things going on in their lives at once.

Boredom and routine drive them crazy. They are driven to keep it fresh by seeking new ideas, experiences, and things. This usually makes them experimental. Geminis tend to take on more than they can handle and be intellectually aggressive. They like to use their words as weapons when they are angry.

Mars in Cancer

Mars in Cancer natives need emotional connections with their partners to fully enjoy the sexual experience. This is a placement for real lovemaking. People with Mars in Cancer are driven by emotion. Family, security, and comfort motivate them. They react emotionally and retreat into their shell when threatened. On the negative side, they can be manipulative and provoke emotional reactions from others.

Mars in Leo

Mars in Leo natives have a strong need to create and be adored. They have the drive to pursue almost anything they want and feel passionate about. These people are romantic and like for sex to feel like worship. They desire to be treated like kings and queens. Mars in Leo natives are very dramatic, aggressive, and demanding when angry.

Mars in Virgo

Mars in Virgo natives are hard workers who strive for perfection. They are always analyzing how they can make the sexual experience and their life better. There is nothing virgin like about this placement. They like sex a whole lot and enjoy pleasing their partners. Mars in Virgo individuals have a strong desire to serve others and tend to nag during difficult times.

Mars in Libra

Mars in Libra natives make great debaters and diplomats. Justice, harmony, and balance are what drive them. Decisiveness is not their strong point. They like to weigh down their options before taking action. Mars in Libra natives like balance in the bedroom. This placement is known for passive aggressiveness. Some Libras turn this energy into action and fight for justice.

Mars in Scorpio

Mars was once known to rule Scorpio. Scorpios are motivated by their high desire to achieve. They have extremely high sex drives and are into exploring taboos. Anything goes with them. Scorpios like to control their lives and dominate in the bedroom. It may take them a while to become angry but when they do, they become vengeful. Sacred sexuality may interest them.

Mars in Ophiuchus a.k.a. Serpentarius

Mars in Ophiuchus natives like to command and dominate during sex. They are intense with high sex drives. Anything goes with them like Scorpio. There are no restrictions or taboos. They are probably polygamous since Ophiuchus is sexually free. Some of them may even be androgynous. Their desire to seek the unknown motivates them. These people can be vengeful and bitter when their buttons are pushed. This is another great placement for practicing sacred sexuality.

Mars in Sagittarius

Mars in Sagittarius natives take a playful, passionate, adventurous, blunt, and fun-loving approach to sex. They are motivated by their strong need to explore and enjoy freedom. These natives may work on many projects at once but don't always follow through. This isn't the most patient placement. They become angry quickly and should find some physical activity to release this energy.

Mars in Capricorn

Mars in Capricorn natives like to be in control of their lives. This includes their sex life. These people are all about using their energy to work hard and achieve goals. They are very sensual like other earth signs. Self-control is strong when it comes to sex, anger, achieving goals, and conserving energy. Capricorns express their anger in a calm and disciplined manner.

Mars in Aquarius

Mars in Aquarius natives come across as detached. Their desire to learn as much as they can motivates them. They like finding new and unconventional ways to accomplish goals. Freedom and individuality are valuable to them. They hate being told what to do. Mars in Aquarius natives are experimental lovers who appreciate mental stimulation in the bedroom. It's hard for them to become angry since they are the most emotionally detached of the zodiac.

Mars in Pisces

Mars in Pisces natives go with the flow and approach life in an indirect manner. They have a poetic outlook and aren't too big on details in the bedroom. Worldly things don't motivate them, which makes it seem like they don't have much drive. They are motivated by higher ideals and causes. Mars in Pisces natives need emotional connections with their partners in the bedroom. They tend to be passive when it comes to sex and expressing anger. These people like to direct their anger inward until they have had enough and explode.

12. JUPITER

Jupiter is the biggest known planet in our solar system and the Roman king of the gods. It is also the planet of luck, wealth, and abundance. Jupiter is very important for choosing careers and manifesting money. The planet of abundance deals with knowledge and expansion since Sagittarius rules it. If you want to find extra ways to make income then Jupiter is one of the places you should look.

Jupiter in Aries

Jupiter in Aries natives will prosper by being innovative, self-sufficient, assertive, courageous, ambitious, and independent. They are meant to be leaders, pioneers, and initiators. This is a good placement for athletes, bosses, entrepreneurs, and people in the military.

Jupiter in Taurus

Jupiter in Taurus natives will attract success and good fortune by being patient and persistent. They can sell goods and be great investors or financial planners. Jupiter in Taurus natives can find work in beauty, the food industry, agriculture, real estate, art, and music.

Jupiter in Gemini

Jupiter in Gemini natives will attract good fortune by using their versatility, social skills, curiosity, intelligence, and knowledge constructively. They can prosper in music, writing, broadcasting, traveling, and teaching. These natives are usually good at multitasking.

Jupiter in Cancer

Jupiter in Cancer natives will attract good fortune when they are sympathetic and giving. They must use their abilities to take care of others and make them feel comfortable. These natives can prosper in real estate, anything that has to do with family, art, and the food industry.

Jupiter in Leo

Jupiter in Leo natives will attract good fortune by creatively expressing themselves and being true leaders. They can prosper in business, entertainment, sports, politics, art, drama, dance, poetry, and music.

Jupiter in Virgo

Jupiter in Virgo natives will prosper by being honest, ethical, structured, orderly, detailed oriented, helpful, and of service to others. Anything dealing with health and healing are a prosperous avenue for them. They can make money as personal trainers, wellness coaches, nutritionists, and plant-based chefs.

Jupiter in Libra

Jupiter in Libra natives will prosper by being fair, cooperative, and diplomatic without being people pleasers. Relationships with others are important. They can find work in art, marketing, law, public relations, beauty, fashion, writing, politics, and counseling.

Jupiter in Scorpio

Jupiter in Scorpio natives will attract prosperity by using their transformative powers and problem solving skills to heal others. They will find success by devoting themselves to one project. These people are interested in deeper studies, taboos, mysteries, and psychology. Jupiter in Scorpio natives can find work as scientists, healers, researchers, detectives, and health professionals.

Jupiter in Ophiuchus a.k.a. Serpentarius

Jupiter in Ophiuchus natives will attract the most fortune when they seek enlightenment and go against the traditional way of doing things. They can prosper as holistic healers, herbalists, dream interpreters, oracles, astrologers, and teachers of sacred knowledge.

Jupiter in Sagittarius

Jupiter is at home in Sagittarius. Sagittarius natives attract good fortune when they are kind, open minded, and practicing what they preach. They value freedom and movement. These people can prosper from traveling, teaching, publishing, and studying foreign cultures.

Jupiter in Capricorn

Jupiter in Capricorn natives will attract good fortune when they are organized, mature, and ethical. Position and status are important to them. They can prosper in fields where they show authority such as being a CEO, boss, entrepreneur, and politician.

Jupiter in Aquarius

Jupiter in Aquarius natives will prosper when they are progressive, humanitarian, inventive, and cooperative. They can make money from social networking, art, humanitarianism, science, inventions, technology, philosophy, and astrology

Jupiter in Pisces

Jupiter in Pisces natives will attract good fortune when they are compassionate and giving. They may volunteer and help the homeless. These people can find work in spirituality, art, metaphysics, and religion. This is a great placement for spiritual teachers and healers.

13. SATURN

Saturn is the planet of limitations, karma, and restrictions. We must look at Saturn to find out what we need to overcome. Saturn is known as the Greek father of the gods. It is an outer planet, so it moves slowly through the zodiac. Capricorn is the disciplinarian of the zodiac and rules Saturn. Challenges make people stronger. They are necessary to develop a higher consciousness.

Saturn in Aries

Saturn in Aries natives must overcome the problems they have dealing with independence, competition, taking initiative, finishing what they start, risk-taking, assertiveness, self-sufficiency, confidence, and drive. Life experiences will force them to develop individuality and self-esteem. They will learn how to be confident and progressive leaders.

Saturn in Taurus

Saturn in Taurus natives must overcome obstacles dealing with values and materials. Life will force them to learn valuable lessons linked to finances and security.

Saturn in Gemini

Saturn in Gemini natives must overcome obstacles dealing with communication and mental abilities. Life experiences will cause them to build supreme mental and communication skills. Seeking knowledge is key.

Saturn in Cancer

Saturn in Cancer natives will face obstacles in life in order to develop a real sense of self-worth. They will learn lessons relating to emotional understanding, emotional expression, and responsibility in regards to family.

Saturn in Leo

Saturn in Leo natives will face challenges in life to develop creative self-expression, confidence, personal power, and control of the ego. They will learn valuable lessons dealing with romantic relationships, leadership, and parenthood.

Saturn in Virgo

Saturn in Virgo natives will be forced to learn organization, discipline, and good planning skills. They will learn lessons dealing with structure, self-improvement, routine, work ethic etc.

Saturn in Libra

Saturn in Libra natives will face obstacles to become experts at human relations on all levels. They will be forced to build a strong sense of responsibility in regards of relationships.

Saturn in Scorpio

Saturn in Scorpio natives will be forced to develop healthy partnerships on emotional and financial levels. Most of their lessons will relate to power, sex, secrets, taboos, intimacy, and shared money. They will learn through many obstacles how to transmute their shadow into light. This placement leads to intense emotional transformation and healing.

Saturn in Ophiuchus a.k.a. Serpentarius

Saturn in Ophiuchus natives will face lessons to test their esoteric knowledge. Do they see beyond the veil and feel beyond the physical? Are they tuning in with the cosmic forces of nature? They may face mistreatment from authorities and courts as consequences for going against social norms. Saturn in Ophiuchus natives will be forced to learn how to use their hidden talents and powers during their mature years.

Saturn in Sagittarius

Saturn in Sagittarius natives will face challenges to have their beliefs tested. Their challenges will most likely be associated with their religious or philosophical views. They will be pushed to become intellectual, optimistic, and enthusiastic about life. Philosophy, religion, and law may interest them.

Saturn in Capricorn

Saturn is in its home Capricorn. Saturn in Capricorn natives will face lessons dealing with business, authority, organization, hard work, and time. They will be forced to develop structure, discipline, persistence, responsibility, work ethic etc. Some of them may have strict fathers or distant relationships with them.

Saturn in Aquarius

Saturn in Aquarius natives will be forced to learn how to be more humanitarian and tolerant when it comes to dealing with people and groups. Obstacles will help them understand human nature and the brotherhood of man. Technology and inventions may interest them.

Saturn in Pisces

Saturn in Pisces natives will be forced to learn valuable lessons relating to boundaries, emotional understanding, compassion, humanity, and a sense of service to others. They will be challenged to learn faith and choose a spiritual path. Spirituality, art, music, and poetry attract them.

14. URANUS

Uranus is associated with Aquarius and originality. It is also linked to the Greek god of the sky. Uranus rules freedom and unexpected changes. This is a generational and outer planet. Therefore, it moves slowly through the zodiac. Uranus takes about 84 years to orbit the sun. It spends between 6-7 years in each sign.

Uranus in Aries

Uranus in Aries generation introduces the pioneering and trailblazing spirit. This generation brought forth innovation in technology, military, science, economics etc. They built high-tech weapons of mass destruction.

Uranus in Taurus

Uranus in Taurus generation brings new ideas concerning material resources. They brought forth innovation in agriculture, economics, the food industry, banking, investments, and the environment.

Uranus in Gemini

Uranus in Gemini generation seeks to bring forth innovations in communication, learning, and technology. They were one of the first generations to go to college in mass.

Uranus in Cancer

Uranus in Cancer generation seeks to bring forth innovations in family life and tradition. They were one of the first generations to change how society viewed families and the role of the traditional housewife.

Uranus in Leo

Uranus in Leo generation brings forth new ideas

about self-expression and individuality. They started sharing their individual gifts with the masses.

Uranus in Virgo

Uranus in Virgo generation brings forth radical changes in healthcare, medicine, and work life in general. They brought the gym culture and organic food shops.

Uranus in Libra

Uranus in Libra generation seeks to bring forth changes in relationships and major partnerships. They revolutionized marriage and made open relationships popular.

Uranus in Scorpio

Uranus in Scorpio generation brings changes to sex, healing, and emotional understanding. They approached sex in an experimental and unusual way. This generation changed the way people related to each other emotionally. AIDS was discovered during this era.

Uranus in Ophiuchus a.k.a. Serpenatarius

Uranus in Ophiuchus generation seeks to bring changes to how society views magical powers, gender, sexuality, and esoteric knowledge. Instant communication transformed their lives. They grew up on video games, e-mail, the Internet, home computers, house phones, and televisions.

Uranus in Sagittarius

Uranus in Sagittarius generation seeks to bring changes to higher education. They think all traditions and beliefs from the past are outdated. This generation values knowledge, philosophy, religion, and spirituality.

Uranus in Capricorn

Uranus in Capricorn generation seeks to bring changes to government and business. They want to establish a brand new social order. This generation made entrepreneurship, self-employment, and freelancing popular.

Uranus in Aquarius

Uranus in Aquarius generation seeks to bring changes to humanity, science, and technology. They want to bring The Scientific Revolution or Age of Enlightenment.

Uranus in Pisces

Uranus in Pisces generation seeks to bring changes to spirituality and religion. They want outdated knowledge to dissolve, so that they can start The Spiritual Revolution.

15. NEPTUNE

Neptune is the planet of confusion, magic, inspiration, hypnosis, visions, dreams, religion, spirituality, and everything that is unseen. This planet is linked to the god of the sea and Pisces. It is also the planet of drugs. Neptune is an outer planet, so that means it moves slowly and generationally through the zodiac. It takes Neptune 165 years to orbit the sun and about 13 years to enter a new sign.

Neptune in Aries

Neptune in Aries generation inspires humanity by introducing new spiritual ideas and philosophy. They idealize independence, freedom, self-sufficiency, and individuality. This generation was born during the Third Great Awakening and era of revivalism. They went to war over spiritual ideas and values.

Neptune in Taurus

Neptune in Taurus generation idealizes business, security, economics, and material resources. They were born towards the end of the second Industrial Revolution.

Neptune in Gemini

Neptune in Gemini generation idealizes education and communication. They used communication for a higher cause by spreading ideas of compassion. Religious literature became popular.

Neptune in Cancer

Neptune in Cancer generation idealizes home and family. They have a vision of a worldly family and take great pride in having a beautiful, well kept home. Neptune in Cancer generation cares about the world as a whole and probably clings to family religion.

Neptune in Leo

Neptune in Leo generation idealizes romance and love. They inspired others through art, dance, glamorous lifestyles, poetry, creative self-expression, fashion, entertainment, film, drama, plays, television etc.

Neptune in Virgo

Neptune in Virgo generation is interested in improving health, employment, and fitness. They have visions of global health and want perfect health available to everyone.

Neptune in Libra

Neptune in Libra generation brings improvement to marriage and commitment. They have visions of ending war and creating lasting world peace. This generation was born during the end of the Civil Rights movement.

Neptune in Scorpio

Neptune in Scorpio generation is interested in sex, emotional connections, and transformative power. They were some of the first people to use sex as an escape. Emotional transformations will lead them to spirituality.

Neptune in Ophiuchus a.k.a. Serpentarius

Neptune in Ophiuchus generation is raising awareness and changing how people perceive the world. They desire to passionately pursue spiritual values and wash away old politics, traditions, ideas, leaders, government systems etc. This generation got to experience both analog and digital technologies.

Neptune in Sagittarius

Neptune in Sagittarius generation brings new spiritual visions of global enlightenment. They will introduce new higher-level concepts of religion, philosophy, and spirituality.

Neptune in Capricorn

Neptune in Capricorn generation brings changes to the material plane. They will wash away old structures of success, work, business, government, and resources.

Neptune in Aquarius

Neptune in Aquarius generation wants to change society and technology. They idealize new ways of interacting with others, independence, and freedom.

Neptune in Pisces

Neptune in Pisces generation idealizes love, religion, compassion, spirituality, creativity, and imagination. They want to spread the message of peace and love.

16. PLUTO

Pluto is the planet of transformation, death, and rebirth. It is linked to the god of the underworld and rules Scorpio. Pluto is all about transforming and rising above lower self-Scorpion ways to higher self-Phoenix ways. Pluto shows where metamorphosis is happening within a person's life. It is an outer and generational planet, so it moves slowly through the zodiac. Pluto takes about 248 years to orbit the sun. It spends between 12-32 years in each sign.

Pluto in Aries

Pluto in Aries generation brings new and transforming ideas. They were seen as the innovative and independent pioneers who overturned society's structures and changed the world. This generation was born during the Civil War and Reconstruction eras.

Pluto in Taurus

Pluto in Taurus generation has a strong desire for material and financial security. They brought great changes to the economy by making things like mass production common.

Pluto in Gemini

Pluto in Gemini generation transforms technology and communication. They are known for inventions and revolutionized communication by creating things like car radios and telephones. Electricity was pioneered as well as the first motored and flying machines.

Pluto in Cancer

Pluto in Cancer generation brings transformative energies to home. They changed the family and home life. This is the generation where women were forced to leave their traditional roles to perform men duties.

Pluto in Leo

Pluto in Leo generation brings changes to creativity, self-expression, romance, and leadership. This generation inspired humanity to open our hearts. They transformed the way the world looked at leadership and power.

Pluto in Virgo

Pluto in Virgo generation brings transformation to healthcare, healing, service, and the environment. They changed the workforce and healthcare. Pluto in Virgo generation wants to conserve natural resources and spread environmental awareness across the globe. Earth day, the Natural Resources Defense Council, and the Environmental Protection Agency were all founded during this era.

Pluto in Libra

Pluto in Libra generation brings transformation to relationships and marriage. They feel like society's ideas of relationships and marriage are outdated. Those born in this generation are focused on justice and creating peace between nations.

Pluto in Scorpio

Pluto in Scorpio generation brings transformation to the emotional plane, sex, and structure. Traumatic experiences were apart of their childhood. Their innocence was taken away at an early age. They will transmute their pain into power, confront the collective shadow, and promote continual personal evolution. Pluto in Scorpio energy urges the world to face the dark side of reality and accept change.

Pluto in Ophiuchus a.k.a. Serpentarius

Pluto in Ophiuchus generation brings transformation to the perception of gender, sex, death, healing, magic, esoteric knowledge, and the unknown. They are known as the "weirdos." Pluto in Ophiuchus energy encourages humanity to transform mentally and physically in order to be reborn.

Pluto in Sagittarius

Pluto in Sagittarius generation brings transformation to religion, beliefs, and education. They are highly interested in travel, culture, law, spirituality, philosophy and higher education.

Pluto in Capricorn

Pluto in Capricorn generation transforms through ambition and structure. They bring big changes to business, world government, power, structure, and the Earth itself. Traditional methods of authority and power will be transformed through violence or destruction.

Pluto in Aquarius

Pluto in Aquarius generation brings transformation to society through original ideas and inventions. Human rights and brotherhood will be fought for. They are likely to cause a breakthrough in the fields of technology, science, and medicine.

Pluto in Pisces

Pluto in Pisces generation seeks transformation through spirituality and religion. They believe in universal love and interconnectedness. This generation changed the way people viewed art, religion, spirituality, and culture.

17. CHIRON

Chiron is known as the "wounded healer." It is a meteor named after the Centaur in Greek mythology. Chiron was a healer who couldn't heal himself, philosopher, astrologer, and oracle. He was also half man and half horse. Looking at Chiron in our natal charts tells us what we need to heal about ourselves. Healing is deep and a lot of the time chaotic.

Chiron in Aries

Chiron in Aries natives need to heal their sense of self. They want to feel accepted. This can cause them to be people pleasers. These individuals may find it hard to stand up for themselves and be individuals since they lack confidence. They probably fear rejection or being judged. Chiron in Aries natives will heal this wound by being their authentic and assertive selves.

Chiron in Taurus

Chiron in Taurus natives must heal their sense of values and self-worth. They probably feel like they never get what they deserve and worry about money excessively. This wound can manifest as poor money management skills and materialism. They feel neglected on all levels. Finding the value within instead of valuing material possessions is key to healing this wound.

Chiron in Gemini

Chiron in Gemini natives must heal wounds dealing with communication and the nervous system. They probably feel like they aren't smart enough and their voice is unheard. Learning how to speak up for themselves and share their truth is key to healing this wound. They must recognize and embrace their own intelligence.

Chiron in Cancer

Chiron in Cancer natives must heal wounds related to emotions, family, and the lack of nurture. They often feel alone, unloved, and abandoned. These people must find love and their true home within to heal from this wound. They will learn to love themselves by discovering that they already have what they need.

Chiron in Leo

Chiron in Leo natives must heal their sense of creative self-expression. They often feel uncreative, uninspired, unimaginative, and unable to express themselves. The key to healing this wound is to live from the heart and see the world as a huge creative project. Once these people gain the confidence to be all that they can be, they will shine and discover their true gifts. They will inspire others to express their creativity.

Chiron in Virgo

Chiron in Virgo natives must heal wounds related to health issues. Their emotions influence their health. They need to learn to discriminate, find order, and realize that nothing is perfect. These natives may feel nervous, critical, and controlling. They must learn to stop being so judgmental. Loving themselves and others for who they are is key to healing this wound.

Chiron in Libra

Chiron in Libra natives must heal how they view relationships. They often feel alone in the world. These people may feel like they need relationships or aren't good enough for them. This placement could lead to people pleasing and commitment issues. Chiron in Libra natives must learn to be whole on their own in order to heal through relationships.

Chiron in Scorpio

Chiron in Scorpio natives will heal wounds related to death, intimate relationships, transformation, and sex. They probably experience dark emotions and build up walls of protection around them. These natives may fear death, change, or loss. Deep introspection, the transmutation of pain to wisdom, and accepting the dark side of reality will help them heal this wound.

Chiron in Ophiuchus a.k.a. Serpentarius

Chiron in Ophiuchus natives must heal wounds related to their inner feminine power, sexuality, and sense of magic. They must also heal from trauma. These people probably feel like outcasts and rejects because of their differences. A lot of them grow up to not like sex that much. Overcoming feelings of shame and the fear of being mistreated for standing out is key.

Chiron in Sagittarius

Chiron in Sagittarius natives must heal wounds dealing with beliefs and spirituality. They have difficulty finding meaning in life and fear going out on adventures. Fear stops them from seeking and enjoying freedom. They will experience at least one transformation of beliefs during their lifetime. Changing how they think and embracing their adventurous nature will help them heal this wound.

Chiron in Capricorn

Chiron in Capricorn natives must heal their sense of responsibility, structure, and authority. They feel unrecognized for their achievements. These people may feel like they can't find their place in the world. Finding and embracing their inner authority is key. They must master and respect themselves in order to heal.

Chiron in Aquarius

Chiron in Aquarius natives must heal their sense of individuality and belonging to a community. They can feel isolated and uncomfortable in groups. These natives are friendly but distant. They probably avoid close relationships too. To heal from this wound, they must look at the bigger picture and embrace being different. Their perspective must shift.

Chiron in Pisces

Chiron in Pisces natives will heal wounds dealing with their sense of spirituality and compassion. They have to learn to create boundaries and share their unique gifts. These natives must heal their relationship with the divine, overcome the fear of betrayal, and let go feelings of victimization. Meditation and solitude can help them heal from this wound.

18. MIDHEAVEN

The midheaven is the highest point in the middle of the heavens during a person's birth. Tropical astrology's location of midheavens is just as inaccurate as the other points. Many know of the midheaven as the point lying on the 10th house cusp but it can also lie on the 9th house cusp. This point indicates a native's status and career throughout life.

The midheaven deals with public image since it is usually on the 10th house, which is the house of status. It describes the kind of business that a person would be into. Midheavens also deal with achievements and how someone will make their mark in the world. They help people choose the best careers for themselves. The tropical system has people working with false midheavens. This is harmful.

Tropical astrology charts say my midheaven is in

Capricorn but I'm not even into corporate work. Plus I don't care for routines. According to 13 sign astrology, my midheaven is in Sagittarius. Sagittarius midheaven makes me a lover of freedom. I need freedom when it comes to choosing a career. Being in an office all day isn't in my nature. Capricorn midheavens like more traditional careers.

Aries Midheaven

Aries midheavens need freedom, challenge, adventure, and excitement in their careers. They may change careers frequently. Routines bore them. Aries midheavens must learn discipline, so that they can follow through and finish what they start. Their strong spirit for independence makes them best suited for self-employment. This is a good placement for entrepreneurs and sports players.

Taurus Midheaven

Taurus midheavens function best in steady and secured careers since they are earth signs. They fear untraditional ways of making money. Careers in banking, art, cooking, singing, real estate, environmental conservation, and gardening may interest them.

Gemini Midheaven

Gemini midheavens need variety and stimulation in their careers. Some of them have 2 careers at the same time. Communication is important in their job field. They can make money from their hands, sales, teaching, writing, the Internet, mass communication etc.

Cancer Midheaven

Cancer midheavens need careers where they can give and receive comfort. These people work best when they are caring for others. They can make money from nursing, working with families, the food industry, real estate, and art.

Leo Midheaven

Leo midheavens like to be the center of attention in the workplace. They are natural born leaders. Careers in acting, music, art, performing, entertainment, business, childcare, and politics may interest them.

Virgo Midheaven

Virgo midheavens want to be of service to others and the planet. Individuals with this placement are organized and practical. They can suffer from perfectionism. Virgo midheavens can prosper in detailed-oriented work like farming, coding, styling, and protecting the environment or health-oriented work like fitness and healthcare.

Libra Midheaven

Libra midheavens are peacemakers. They need peace and harmony in the workplace. Careers in law, beauty, fashion, counseling, and art will work best for them.

Scorpio Midheaven

Scorpio midheavens have to be emotionally involved with their career in order for it to work. They are problem solvers and truth seekers. Careers in detective work, research, healing, the medical field, psychology, science, and the funeral industry may suit them.

Ophiuchus a.k.a. Serpentarius Midheaven

Ophiuchus midheavens are outcasts. They can prosper in holistic medicine and be the greatest healers. Their limitless knowledge of science can make them great teachers, astrologers, oracles, and dream interpreters as well.

Sagittarius Midheaven

Sagittarius midheavens need freedom when it comes to choosing careers. They probably have 2 or more careers. These people love to be challenged and hate routine. They can find careers in sports, sales, travel, religion, spirituality, philosophy, the space industry, teaching, publishing etc.

Capricorn Midheaven

Capricorn midheavens need practical, orderly, and structured careers. These natives want to achieve as much they possibly can. Status and public image are important to them. They can find careers in self-employment, politics, management, business etc. This is the perfect placement for a CEO or businessperson.

Aquarius Midheaven

Aquarius midheavens need freedom and the ability to be innovative in their careers. Since Uranus rules Aquarius, they may change careers 1 or more times. They can invent things. Careers in science, research, humanitarianism, technology, self-employment, social networking, and astrology suit them.

Pisces Midheaven

Pisces midheavens like to follow their intuition when it comes to careers. They are compassionate, inspirational, and spiritual. These people can make great counselors. The Fish need variety. This makes them versatile. They can prosper in music, art, film, poetry, spirituality, philosophy, religion, healing, and anything dealing with helping others.

19. USING THE ZODIAC TO MANIFEST

A lot of people limit themselves to one sign but we are all of the signs. It's time we learn how to use the energy of each sign to navigate through the matrix more effectively and manifest greater lives. Aries energy urges us to be individuals, initiate things, pioneer, and fearlessly fight for what we believe in. Taurus energy teaches us how to stay persistent, ground ourselves, make money, and survive. Gemini energy inspires us to communicate, embrace our inner child, trade, and be versatile. Cancer energy helps us nurture, tune in with our feelings, create strong families, and build homes. Leo energy inspires us to lead, express ourselves, and shine confidently. Virgo energy urges us to serve, take care of our health, improve our lifestyles, and perfect our work.

Libra energy inspires us to appreciate life's beauty, seek peace, cooperate, and balance our relationships.

Scorpio energy teaches us to dig deeply for truth, embrace our power, tap into the unknown, transform, and create everlasting bonds with others. Ophiuchus energy urges us to heal holistically, raise our kundalini (life force) energy up our spines, and balance our chakras. Sagittarius energy gives us vision and inspires us to explore infinite possibilities. Capricorn energy teaches us to patiently work hard towards long-term goals and build structure.

Aquarius energy urges us to be innovative, detached, progressive, unique, humanitarian, and scientific. Pisces energy teaches us to be united as one, compassionate, inspiring, artistic, and imaginative. Everyone should work with constellations. The stars are alive, so it makes sense to share our intentions with them. All of us are lacking in some way. We must study all of the signs and master the energies that we lack.

20. COMPATIBILITY

"His sign is Capricorn. I'm a Sagittarius. We are incompatible." It's always funny hearing people base compatibility on sun signs. It takes more than sun signs to see if 2 people are compatible. We have to look at the other celestial objects in people's natal charts as well. The sun is in the wrong position according to mainstream astrology, so we know the other celestial objects are in the wrong place too.

We have to look at the sun, moon, Mars, and Venus based on 13 sign astrology to truly determine compatibility. In a man's chart, his Venus and moon are more important than the sun when it comes to attraction. It's because the moon and Venus are both feminine. Since men are masculine at the core, this feminine energy is projected outward. It is the energy that he desires from a woman.

For instance, a Gemini moon man is attracted to a woman he can talk to about anything. She has to stimulate his mind or he will be bored. If his Venus is in Leo, he wants a confident, classy, sophisticated, and outgoing lover. The woman who stands out from the crowd catches his attention. She is most likely bossy too.

In a woman's chart, her sun and Mars are important when it comes to attraction. The sun and Mars both deal with masculine energy. Since women are feminine at the core, this energy is projected outward. She desires this energy from her masculine counterpart.

A Taurus sun woman probably wants someone on her level materially or better. With Mars in Aries, she prefers men who are independent, direct, and strong. This type of woman is probably attracted to athletes or adventurers. She likes driven and action-oriented men. The moon can play a factor too. Virgo moon women are attracted to healthy men who are eager to provide for them.

The more advanced way to calculate compatibility is to merge the natal charts of two people. This is known as composite astrology. The points are found by calculating the midpoint between each planet and point of 2 individuals. Combined points are called composite points.

A composite sun in Aquarius couple comes across as intellectual and unconventional. They may share humanitarian values and believe that social networking is important. Both people need freedom to change. They might enjoy going out together and attracting people with their stimulating conversation.

A composite Sagittarius moon couple needs freedom to explore. They are adventurous and optimistic. Others come to them when they need uplifting. This is the type of couple to enjoy traveling and broadening their horizons together.

Composite Mars in Aries couples are ready to make their mark in the world and conquer every challenge that they meet. Together, they are more confident and expressive. They are raw with a lot of energy that can turn into aggression if they don't use it constructively. This energy should be used to exercise and play sports together. Their sex is straightforward and passionate.

A composite Venus in Gemini couple loves communicating and expressing themselves within their relationship. They feel like they can talk to one another about anything. Maintaining a strong emotional connection is key since the couple takes a logical and intellectual approach towards their relationship. Composite astrology works for business relationships, family, and friendships as well.

21. BUSINESS ASTROLOGY

The wealthy use astrology all the time. They are aware of the power the stars have on our everyday lives. A lot of corporations use new and full moons to host their events. Special moon phases make people more sensitive, emotional, attractive, and easier to manipulate. Anyone can use new and full moons to attract abundance. It's best to start projects during the new moon since it begins a new cycle. New moons grow to symbolize growth and full moons shrink to symbolize letting go.

It's important to start businesses and projects on special days at special times. Businesses are entities, which mean they have their own star signs. I started my 13 sign astrology business on January 1st, 2017 at 11:38 am. It is a Sagittarius sun and midheaven. This was a great time to start my career since Sagittarius rules higher learning and is also my midheaven. Midheavens deal with careers. I was born at 1:38 am, so I couldn't have chosen a more significant time to start my astrological business. Business has been flourishing since.

My Mars is in Taurus. Mars is the planet of sex and Taurus is a sensual sign. I'm very sensual with a high sex drive. It's a good placement for anyone interested in practicing sacred sexuality. I wrote a book on men's sexual health and released it back in April-May 2017 when Mars was in Taurus. The books are still selling.

Apple was founded on April 1st. This makes it a Pisces. Pisces deals with the collective consciousness. It makes sense why the collective has been going crazy over Apple since it came out. Apple's fans are basically a cult. Pisces deals with glamour too, which is why Apple products are so attractive to the eyes. Steve Jobs was born on February 24th. He is an inventive Aquarius sun. Apple needed Steve's inventiveness. He created the I-phone, which changed many lives today. Look at Apple since Steve passed on. They haven't changed the I-phone around as much as they should have.

Most people know July 4th as Independence Day but it is really a special time where our sun is aligned with its sun Sirius. Ancient civilizations celebrated this special planetary alignment for thousands of millennia. The Founding Fathers knew this and used astrology to the best of their advantage. America is a Mercury ruled Gemini. Mercury is a trickster, so it makes sense why the USA is filled with con artists.

Amazon was founded on July 5th. Therefore, Amazon is a Gemini sun. It deals with mercurial things like trade, the Internet, technology, communication, and commerce. Amazon is a giant e-commerce business that is changing the way the world shops. Its versatility is killing thousands of companies.

Twitter was founded on March 21st. This is the beginning of the spring equinox. It's also when the sun is in Pisces. Pisces deals with duality, confusion, deception, spirituality, collective consciousness, unconsciousness, religion etc. Twitter is filled with false spirituality, duality, ultra sensitivity, and confusion. There are plenty of fake gurus and overly sensitive people on Twitter. It's full of deceivers. Many are even joining cults unknowingly. On the other hand, there is some good information and journalism on Twitter. Twitter is a way to observe collective consciousness. It connects people from all over the world.

Instagram was founded in October. October is Virgo season. Virgo deals with detailed and visual work. Instagram is a place where anyone can post pictures. It's visual. People like to use Instagram to advertise their modeling abilities and photography. Many just use it to boost their egos while others make a living from it.

Choosing when to start a project or business is just as important as choosing a name. Are you writing a book or building a website? Release it when the sun is in Gemini, Libra, or Aquarius. Air signs rules the Internet, technology, writing, and communication. Do you desire to start your own restaurant? Open it during Taurus, Capricorn, or Virgo season. Earth signs rule the senses.

Are you interested in building businesses that revolve around creativity, spirituality, or helping others? Initiate them during Cancer, Scorpio, or Pisces season. Water signs deal with creativity, spirituality, and helping others. Do you want to start a travel, management, or sports type business? Launch it during Aries, Leo, or Sagittarius season. Fire signs deal with freedom, travel, entrepreneurship, and sports.

Have you thought about building businesses based on

ancient secrets and holistic healing? Start them during Scorpio or Ophiuchus season. Watery Scorpio and ethereal Ophiuchus both deal with the occult and healing. Marriage counseling and therapy type businesses should launch during Libra, Cancer, or Pisces season. They all have something to do with romance and helping other people.

22. NATAL CHARTS

The word natal relates to the time or place of someone's birth. Mainstream astrology natal charts don't match the planetary alignments during a person's birth. They don't have anything to do with a person's birth time or place. This goes against the whole meaning of natal charts, which makes them deceitful. Authentic natal charts consist of signs that are all different shapes and sizes. They include the 12 known signs plus Ophiuchus since they document real time and planetary movements.

Working with 13 sign natal charts help one maneuver through the matrix more effectively than others. They give people a clearer understanding of their role in the universe and can be used as road maps. If people actually had to use natal charts to reach their destinations, most would be lost since their road maps are inaccurate. Many are working with fraud sky maps but believe they are going somewhere. They are stuck in a false reality on artificial time. Their fake natal charts don't have anything to do with their lives or the heavens.

Legit natal charts point out wounds that need to be healed, ways emotions are expressed, motivations, career choices, gifts, reincarnation lessons, soul mates, strengths, weaknesses, communication style etc. To read a natal chart, one must first understand the language of symbols. Study the symbols of signs, planets, and other points. After that, one needs to learn about the different houses and aspects. The only way to get a real natal chart reading is to book a 13 sign astrologer like myself for natal chart reading services. Most websites are generating inaccurate natal charts 24/7, which is why they are free. You get what you pay for. My astrological services can be found at

www.babylonisburnin.com.

23. HOUSES

There are traditionally 12 houses in the zodiac. However, some astrologers work with 13. Tropical astrologers believe that each house is the same amount of degrees as the signs and they couldn't be more inaccurate. This is why some houses, according to 13 sign astrology, have 2 or more signs in them. Houses are homes to different zodiac signs. When planets enter a house, they reflect the energies of the sign ruled by that house.

Aries and Mars rule the 1st house. It deals with how people view themselves. The 1st house has a relationship with the ascendant. It's the 1st thing that people see when they meet someone. Let's say Mars is at home in someone's 1st house. This person is seen as aggressive, competitive, impulsive, adventurous, confident, assertive, independent, and sexual.

Taurus and Venus rule the 2nd house. This house deals with the material plane. It is the house of wealth and values. Planets in the 2nd house say a lot about a person's values. The 2nd house is a good place to look at if you want to make some extra money.

Mercury is the planet of trade and commerce. Mercury in the 2nd house would make a person value learning and sharing information. It makes them very crafty in the ways that they make a living. Mercury rules Gemini, so they can make money from Gemini things like e-commerce, writing, working in the media, programming, distributing information etc. Their mental and communicative abilities will help them gain wealth.

Gemini and Mercury rule the 3rd house. It deals with things like learning, communication, community, short travel, siblings etc. Moon in 3rd house natives feel fulfilled on an emotional level when they communicate, learn, and gain knowledge. Mental stimulation is important to them.

Cancer and the moon rule the 4th house. Venus in 4th house natives love their roots. They like for relationships in their home to be beautiful and harmonious. Like a Cancer, they can be clingy in love. Venus in 4th house natives probably enjoy staying home more than going out.

Leo and the sun rule the 5th house. It deals with creativity, self-expression, and romance. Chiron in 5th house natives must heal their sense of creative self-expression. They can do this by picking up new hobbies. These natives may be shy. Becoming confident enough to seek their gifts and express them is key to their healing.

Virgo rules the 6th house. It is the home of Mercury. The 6th house deals with work, routine, and health. Sun in the 6th house makes work, routine, and health important in a person's everyday life. These people are usually hardworking and somewhat health conscious. They can suffer from perfectionism and being workaholics.

Libra and Venus rule the 7th house. It is the house of relationships. Someone with Jupiter in the 7th house would develop their philosophies and grow through relationships. It is also the house of marriage, so having a lot of planets here symbolizes a strong chance of getting married.

The 8th house is the home of Scorpio and Pluto. It is associated with death, sex, and transformation. The 8th house deals with shared money and resources. Mars in 8th house natives have strong sex drives and may face power struggles in intense relationships. They like to seek out joint ventures. Some people with this placement may have suffered from sexual abuse at some point during their lives.

Ophiuchus' natural house is always between the 8th and 9th house since it is a blend of Scorpio and Sagittarius. You can consider it house 8.5.

Sagittarius rules the 9th house. The 9th house deals with Jupiter and expansion. It is the house of higher learning and philosophy. A person with Uranus in the 9th house has unusual and original philosophies. Their unorthodox views make them somewhat rebellious.

Capricorn and Saturn rule the 10th house. The 10th house is the home of careers, status, and public image. Planets in the 10th house are often symbols of success in life. Sun in 10th house natives identify with their career and status. Their reputation is important.

The 11th house is home to Uranus and Aquarius. It deals with groups of people and friendships. Venus in 11th house natives love working in groups and bringing people together. They may even be a part of some artistic and unusual groups. These natives are attracted to unique individuals. Making friends and networking comes easily to them. They are most likely popular.

Pisces and Neptune rule the 12th house. The 12th house is the home of spirituality, seclusion, collective consciousness, unconsciousness, hidden enemies, self-sacrifice, mysticism, religion, confusion, illusions, deception etc. Saturn in 12th house natives will face difficulties and limitations dealing with their unconscious minds. These natives may suffer from low self-esteem and anxiety. They feel responsible for things they can't control. This creates guilt. Their dads may be absent or distant since Saturn deals with father figures. They must learn to accept loneliness and let go emotionally. Saturn in 12th house can lead to isolation, insecurities, fear, escapism, and depression.

24. ASTROLOGICAL TRANSITS

When we speak on transits, we speak on the positions of the planetary objects. Since the tropical system isn't star based, the transits are wrong. Tropical fanatics are never right when they say a celestial object is at a certain place at a certain time. When the average person says, "The moon is in Capricorn," they really mean the moon is in the Sagittarius constellation. Like I've explained in the previously chapters, tropical astrology is off 28 degrees (one complete moon cycle) or one whole sign.

It's important to work with real transits, so we can tune in with real universal energies. Transits help us predict how we will be influenced. Horoscopes are determined by transits. Break down the word horoscope and you get "observer of time." Mainstream horoscopes are false observers of time. They are not based on true planetary movements. Working with fake transits is setting one up for failure. The heavens are alive and always changing.

It's called a transit when the sun moves from Pisces to Aquarius and when Mercury moves from Taurus to Gemini. Sun in Aquarius transits encourage us to be social and create more meaningful connections as well as fulfill our hunger for knowledge. Mercury in Pisces transits open up our minds to infinite realms and increase our intuition. Moon in Ophiuchus transits motivate us to perform energy healing and raise the kundalini (life force) up our spines to our crowns.

Some people like to get transit readings. Transit readings compare birth charts with the current, future, or past sky. Let's say your birthday is February 15th, 1978. You can compare your birth chart to February 13th, 2018 or February 10th, 1979. It's all up to you and what you want to figure out.

25. THE TRUE ASTROLOGICAL AGE

People always say "We are in the age of Aquarius" but this is incorrect like most things people say about astrology. Tropical astrology has all the planetary movements wrong, so we should know the astrological age is wrong as well. Where are the new systems, information, inventions, and sciences? It's a fake new age. We are still in the Age of Pisces where people fail to balance science and spirituality.

Aquarius deals with truth and enlightenment. The Age of Aquarius will make us truth seekers and researchers. Today, ignorance is more abundant than knowledge. People wouldn't follow fake stars or have problems distinguishing facts from misinformation if we were in the Age of Information. Unfortunately, this is the Age of Misinformation. Nothing should be taken for truth without further investigation and research.

Pisces deals with spirituality, duality, religion, illusions, deception, and the unseen. The Age of Pisces is also the Age of Religion. It's the period of time when Christianity, Buddhism, and Islam first began to emerge. Religious fanaticism is at an all time high today. Even though religion was not created to control people, world rulers have used it as a tool of control throughout history.

Deception is coming from every direction in the Age of Pisces. False spirituality and fake bodies are everywhere. A lot of lies are being told in the media to manipulate and mislead the masses. Everyone from the pope to the government uses weapons of mass deception. The world is under mind control. Reality TV isn't reality. Fluoride is in the water. The food most eat is poison. Hospitals are killing people. Drugs don't cure anyone. People are using drugs as an attempt to escape their reality. The food and drug industry have a hidden connection that makes both a lot of money. The concept of time mostly used is an illusion. Modern day education revolves around many lies. The Age of Aquarius will bring truth and end all deception.

Earth is tilting on its axis. This is called the precession of the equinoxes. It's one reason the sky appears to be changing and the spring (or vernal) equinox arrives earlier than the previous years. Mainstream astrology fanatics believe we are in the Age of Aquarius but think Aries starts spring. According to their logic, it would be the Age of Aries. In reality, the Age of Aries was several millennia ago. It was when the world started seeking individuality. Egos and tribal wars were the outcome.

We are not in the Age of Aries or the Age of Aquarius. This is actually the great age in between them. Currently, Pisces starts spring, which makes it the Age of

Pisces for about 500-600 more years. That's when the sun will enter Aquarius to start spring and usher in the new Age of Aquarius. Earth's current population will be dead by then.

Biblical stories say Christ fed 5000 people with 2 fish and 5 loaves of bread. This is a metaphor for astrology. Christ symbolizes the sun and the 2 fish represent Pisces. He even calls his disciples "fishers of men." Fish also represent Christianity. Popes wear fish shaped hats.

The 2 fish symbolize the harmonious energies of yin and yang. The 5 loaves of bread represent the 5 elements of nature, which are manifestations of yin and yang. Christ's mother was a Virgin or Virgo. Virgo and Pisces are opposite signs. His birth marked the end of the age of Aries and the beginning of the Age of Pisces. We have been in the Age of Pisces for more than 2000 years now.

The Age of Pisces is urging us to question our beliefs

in order to perfect them, build faith, achieve balance, overcome materialism, love unconditionally, and figure out the origin of humanity. Nobody's beliefs are perfect. People are still battling over religion and separating astrology from astronomy. They even debate religion versus spirituality like the 2 can't coexist. Many are clinging to isms and creating more division instead of seeing the divinity in all that exists. This wouldn't happen in the Age of Aquarius because we would value love, brotherhood, knowledge, and unity. Building universal belief systems will help humanity overcome our differences and serve each other.

The shift in the cosmos is influencing everyone and everything. Humanity must make the transition to star based astrology and evolve with nature. We are at the end of a cycle. Tune into the cosmos and witness the resurrection of Ophiuchus (Christ).

BIBLIOGRAPHY

Aubin, Ada, and June Rifkin. *The Complete Book of Astrology*. Saint Martin's Press, 1998.

Avery, Jeanne. *The Rising Sign: Your Astrological Mask*. Broadway Books, 2001.

Beck, Roger Lyne. *A Brief History of Ancient Astrology*. Blackwell Publishing, 2006.

Berg, Walter. *The Thirteen Signs of the Zodiac*. Thorsons, 1995.

Burk, Kevin. *Astrology: Understanding the Birth Chart:a Comprehensive Guide to Classical Interpretation*. Llewellyn Publications, 2003.

Collins, Gene. *Cosmopsychology: the Psychology of Humans as Spiritual Beings*. Xlibris Corp, 2009.

Das, Shiva. *Divine Love Astrology: Revealing Spiritual*

Truth for Personal Transformation. North Atlantic Books, 2014.

Galloway, Thomas, and Augustus De Morgan. *Precession of the Equinoxes*. A. And C. Black, 1842.

Golder, Carole. *Moon Signs for Lovers: an Astrological Guide to Perfect Relationships*. Holt, 1992.

Goodman, Linda. *Linda Goodman's Star Signs*. PAN Books, 2016.

INC., RawGoddess. "13 Signs: New Moon in Pisces. . . . .Mamiwata Returns." *RAW GODDESS, INC.*, 15 Apr. 2018, rawgoddessinc.wordpress.com/.

Kent, April Elliott. *Astrological Transits: the Beginner's Guide to Using Planetary Cycles to Plan and Predict Your Day, Week, Year (or Destiny)*. Fair Winds

Press, 2015.

Levine, Joyce. *Breakthrough Astrology: Transform Yourself and Your World*. Weiser Books, 2006.

Miller, Natalie. "The Moon in the 13 Signs." *13 Sign Astrology for All*, 2017, siderealist.com/natalie-13moons.html.

Murray, Margaret Alice. *Ancient Egyptian Legends*. J. Murray, 1913.

Ortleb, Edward P., and Richard Cadice. *The Solar System*. Milliken Pub. Co., 1986.

Osei-Ghansah, Kwame. *The 13th Zodiac (Ophiuchus) and the Galactic Solar System Unveiled*. AuthorHouse, 2006.

Paterson, Helena, et al. *The Handbook of Celtic Astrology: the 13-Sign Lunar Zodiac of the Ancient*

Druids. Llewellyn, 1998.

Powell, Robert. *Chronicle of the Living Christ: the Life and Ministry of Jesus Christ: Foundations of Cosmic Christianity*. Anthroposophic Press, 1996.

Read, Regina Atara. *13 Sun Signs of the Zodiac A.k.a. the Zodiac Conspiracy*. Xlibris Corp, 2014.

Rowe, Anne, and Donald Harley. *The Secret Name of Ra*. Rigby Interactive Library, 1996.

Saulnier, Melissa. *FALLEN RACE: the Inheritance*. Lulu Com, 2018.

Stewart, J. V. *Astrology: What's Really in the Stars*. Prometheus Books, 1996.

Stray, Geoff. *Beyond 2012: Catastrophe or Awakening?: a Complete Guide to End-of-Time Predictions*. Bear & Company, 2009.

Tubb, Kristin O'Donnell. *The 13th Sign*. Square Fish, 2014.

ABOUT THE AUTHOR

In 2017, Ezekiel Brumfield Jr. published his book *Heal-Thy Sex Life: For Men*. It would later become the first of many. Ezekiel was born in New Orleans, Louisiana on July 9th, 1994. Zeke is an entrepreneur, self-published author, self-taught astronomer, blogger, health enthusiast, and the founder of babylonisburnin.com. He loves learning the truth about everything and sharing it with others. Ezekiel is an energetic, witty, self-reliant, and curious 24 year old who enjoys stargazing, studying the universe, walking in nature, reading, writing, talking about current events, eating natural food etc. He uses his communicative and mental abilities to write informative books.

www.ingramcontent.com/pod-product-compliance
Lightning Source LLC
Chambersburg PA
CBHW070641300426
44111CB00013B/2207